IMAGES
of America

THE LITTLE GREENBRIER SCHOOL

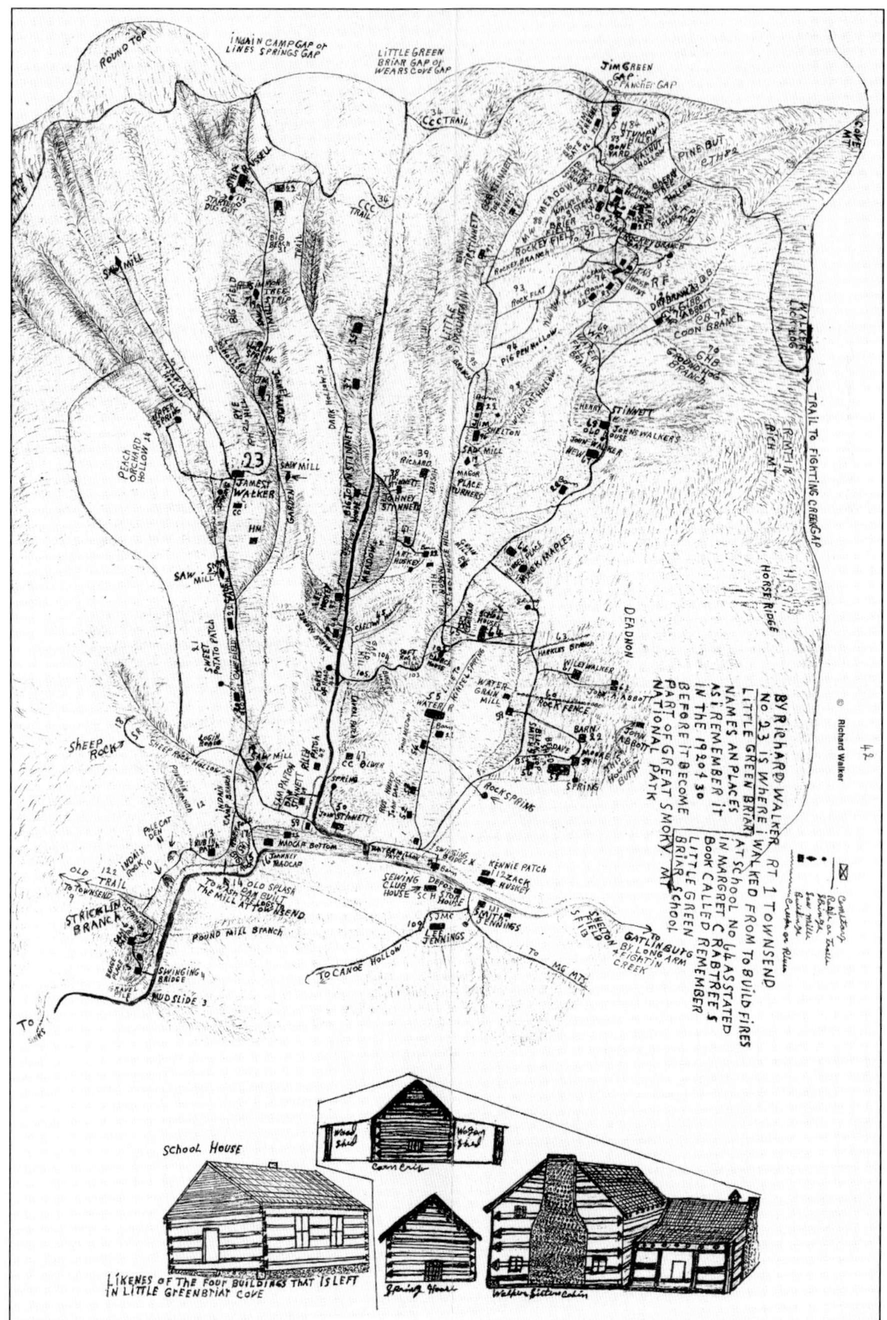

Richard Walker drew this map of the Little Greenbrier community outlining where homesteads and landmarks were located. Note the different buildings in Metcalf Bottoms. (Courtesy Great Smoky Mountains National Park archives.)

ON THE COVER: This photograph was taken by E.E. Exline in March 1936 on the last day of regular classes at the Little Greenbrier School. Even though the children appear to be happy, they would never again go to school together as classmates. (Courtesy Great Smoky Mountains National Park archives.)

IMAGES
of America

The Little Greenbrier School

Karen Rowe Paulin

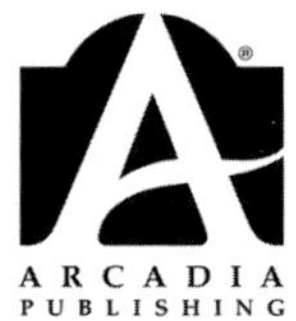

ISBN 978-1-4671-0753-2

Published by Arcadia Publishing
Charleston, South Carolina

Printed in the United States of America

Library of Congress Control Number: 2021943008

For all general information, please contact Arcadia Publishing:
Telephone 843-853-2070
Fax 843-853-0044
E-mail sales@arcadiapublishing.com
For customer service and orders:
Toll-Free 1-888-313-2665

Visit us on the Internet at www.arcadiapublishing.com

This book is dedicated to my husband, Daniel Lee Paulin, and our daughters Sarah Meredith and Corey Botsford. We vacationed so many times in the Great Smoky Mountains area while living in Indiana that we decided—with our daughters' blessing—to move here when we retired. This book is also dedicated to my wonderful grandsons Andrew, Luke, and Garrett Botsford, who remind me to see the world through a child's eyes.

Contents

ACKNOWLEDGMENTS

Thank you so very much to my editor and partner in crime, my husband, Daniel Paulin, for his never-ending assistance with this book.

Robin Goddard presents the Great Smoky Mountains National Park's program at the Little Greenbrier School every Tuesday from mid-April to the end of October. I have had the privilege of hearing her programs and picking her brain for many years, having been a volunteer at the Little Greenbrier School.

Jean Teaster and Tina Becker provided me with images for this book.

Michael Aday at the National Park Service Collections Preservation Center helped so much in gathering articles, manuscripts, and pictures for me to peruse and use.

Without the help of my friend Louis Claudio, I would not have had some of the pictures in the book.

Thank you to the staff members of the Blount County Library, McClung Library, Anna Porter Library, King Family Library, and Pigeon Forge Library for all their assistance in finding information.

Finally, thank you to all the visitors who come to the area. You spark my interest with your many questions and comments.

Introduction

Four walls, one roof, four windows, one door—a very simple layout, but oh, what those walls have seen. At the time of this writing in 2021, the Little Greenbrier School building has been around for approximately 140 years and counting, and many events have taken place over those years.

A volunteer in the park at the Little Greenbrier School is the first person a visitor talks to and asks questions. One of the first usually is: Why on earth did "they" build a church/school out here in the middle of nowhere? The fact is that much was out in the middle of nowhere in the early 1800s, and Tennessee was a wild frontier.

In the late 1700s and early 1800s, as the East Coast became more populated and much too crowded for some adventurous souls, the push west began expanding into the Appalachians. Some settlers, as most people well know, kept going west, but many set up permanent residences along the way that Daniel Boone, and later Meriwether Lewis and William Clark, had opened up through the frontier.

Game was plentiful, and trees were available for buildings and fuel. Streams provided food and water for homesteaders. In this seemingly perfect place, home bases were established by several families near Little Greenbrier. One of these was the Renfro family.

John Renfro acquired 2,000 acres as part of a land grant. He sold 400 acres to Brice McFalls in 1838. McFalls built a small cabin on his tract, which was later added to the Walker "big house" for use as a kitchen. In 1853, another 205 acres were sold to William Richardson, whose heirs sold the land to Wylie King.

In 1857, Wylie and Margaret King built their home in the Little Greenbrier area approximately 1.1 miles from where the Little Greenbrier School is now. After Wylie King passed away, it became evident that Margaret needed assistance with the homestead. Her daughter, also named Margaret, and her son-in-law John N. Walker moved in with her along with two of Margaret and John's sons who were born in Buckeye, Tennessee. Over the coming years, the homestead came to be known as the Walker cabin.

John N. (the "N" stood for "no middle name") Walker was the patriarch of the Little Greenbrier community. He suggested that they needed a school where children could learn and a church where the people could worship in the Primitive Baptist faith. He contacted Sevier County officials, who said they would support his request for a school and provide the teacher if the community could erect a suitable building.

Ephraim Ogle donated logs for the building, and William Gilbert Abbott donated approximately two acres that were reasonably flat for the site. After the logs were sufficiently seasoned, construction started in 1881. As was the practice at the time, the dragging of the logs by oxen required the ground to be frozen so the job would be easier.

Cornermen John W. Walker, Ephraim Ogle, Gilbert Abbott, and Henry Clabo—along with James Thomas Walker, Bill Stinnett, and Bill Watson—constructed the school with the help of the community.

When the huge poplar logs reached the site, the hard work began. The logs were split down the middle, then twice down the side of the initial split. These two large pieces were used as matching walls on the east and west sides, and the same was done for the north and south sides. The remaining sides of the log were used for benches and puncheon flooring. Five large logs were used for the east and west sides, and five were used for the north and south sides. With men on the inside and outside of the building, placement of the logs began. The ends were dovetailed—no screws or nails were used in the construction. When a perfect rectangle was completed five logs high, the door and windows were cut out. An auger was used beside the door opening to bore a hole all the way down to the bottom log. A dogwood tree was inserted into the hole to provide stability for the walls.

The school was described in a Historic American Buildings Survey (HABS) report as:

> One story log structure 24' x 30' built from poplar logs averaging 24" in width. The building is five logs high and made from matched logs split on the site. The roof is of the gable type with pole rafters and covered with split oak shingles. The building has a puncheon floor made from poplar logs three to four inches thick. There are two windows on each side and a door at the front. The foundation is made from loose piled rocks. Its appearance has changed very little since its construction. At one time there was a small window at the back of the building to provide light for the teacher's desk; this has since been boarded over. Maintenance, since the park acquired the building, has consisted of replacing deteriorated sections as needed. All replacement has been with native materials as close to the original as possible.

Sevier County provided the teacher for the first school session, which began on January 1, 1882. School initially lasted for six weeks to two months and was held in the winter only, as the children were needed at home the rest of the year to assist with farm chores.

Clearing of the land by removing rocks and trees, along with planting, occupied children in the spring. Maintenance of the farm was required in summer. Reaping the fruits and vegetables and preparing meat for storage was the focus of the fall. The more food a farm produced and stored, the more the family was able to eat throughout the year. Cabbage was made into sauerkraut. Fruit was either dried or made into jams and jellies. Green beans were strung to make "leather britches." Other vegetables were dried on racks and stored in crocks. Springhouses, crocks, and rafters were the main areas used for storing produce.

Once winter came and school began, it was time for students to learn the four subjects of arithmetic, spelling, reading, and handwriting. Richard Perryman was the first teacher at Little Greenbrier School. A list of all the teachers who worked at the school can be found on page 93.

In *The Gentle Winds of Change, a History of Sevier County, Tennessee, 1900–1930*, the Smoky Mountain Historical Society writes:

> Since there was virtually no funding from the state and very little county support of schools, Sevier Countians had to rely on a number of methods to educate their children. The public schools were supported almost entirely by their respective communities. Frequently the county government donated building supplies to a community if the men of that community donated their labor to build the school. Often a church building was used for a schoolhouse on weekdays. . . . In spite of many people's fond memories of their teachers, the root of the problem appears to have been with them. To be sure, salaries were pitifully low, the school year (even when it was lengthened to five months) was much too short, and materials for the classroom were in shockingly short supply. Yet at bottom, many of these teachers were not well trained and were given no incentive to improve their own knowledge. It is even possible that a few kept the students' progress slow, so that the subscription schools would continue to do a lively business. As far as the State of Tennessee was concerned (according to a certificate from the State Department of Education dated July 15, 1915), it was more important that a teacher was "a person of good moral character who does not use intoxicants, opiates, or cigarettes" than it was that

> he or she be highly qualified academically. Most teachers had graduated from the eighth grade and had passed a state examination, although some were allowed to teach any grade which they themselves had passed.

Education reform went into full swing in the early 1900s. Compulsory attendance laws were enacted in 1909. An eighth-grade graduation certificate came about in 1912. Required school days per year were increased to 160 in 1926.

On August 26, 1933, the Tennessee Park Commission purchased the school property from the Sevier County Board of Education while the commission was acquiring land to form the Great Smoky Mountains National Park.

All of these changes ended up contributing to the end of the Little Greenbrier School as a place for the education of children, but the coming of the national park took care of what seemed to be problem areas, such as compulsory attendance, days required to attend school, and funding, when the school closed for good in the spring of 1936.

One

Who Made It Possible

If it were not for two men, James Shelton and E.E. Exline, there would be very few photographic records of the history of Little Greenbrier.

Edouard Evartt Exline, a landscape architect by profession, was an amateur photographer of great talent. He documented events for the National Park Service and the Civilian Conservation Corps, and also searched for scenic subjects in the area on his own.

James "Jim" Shelton focused on the Little Greenbrier area, his logging work, and the Walker family, into which he married.

In Carroll McMahan's book *Upland Chronicles of the Smokies*, an article on Jim Shelton states,

> Before he and Caroline married, Jim became interested in photography. His equipment was a bulky bellows camera with rectilinear lens. The camera made negatives on glass plates five by eleven inches in size. Jim often boasted that his camera was one of the best ever made, had the best set of shutters on it that squeezed the bulb to make an exposure and it had three track bellows that focused on whatever he wanted to shoot. Carrying his heavy equipment, Jim climbed knobs and leaped from boulder to boulder to cross creeks to record a picture history of the Smoky Mountains. . . . He developed his pictures in a crude darkroom he built that included a spring fed through which he used to process his images.

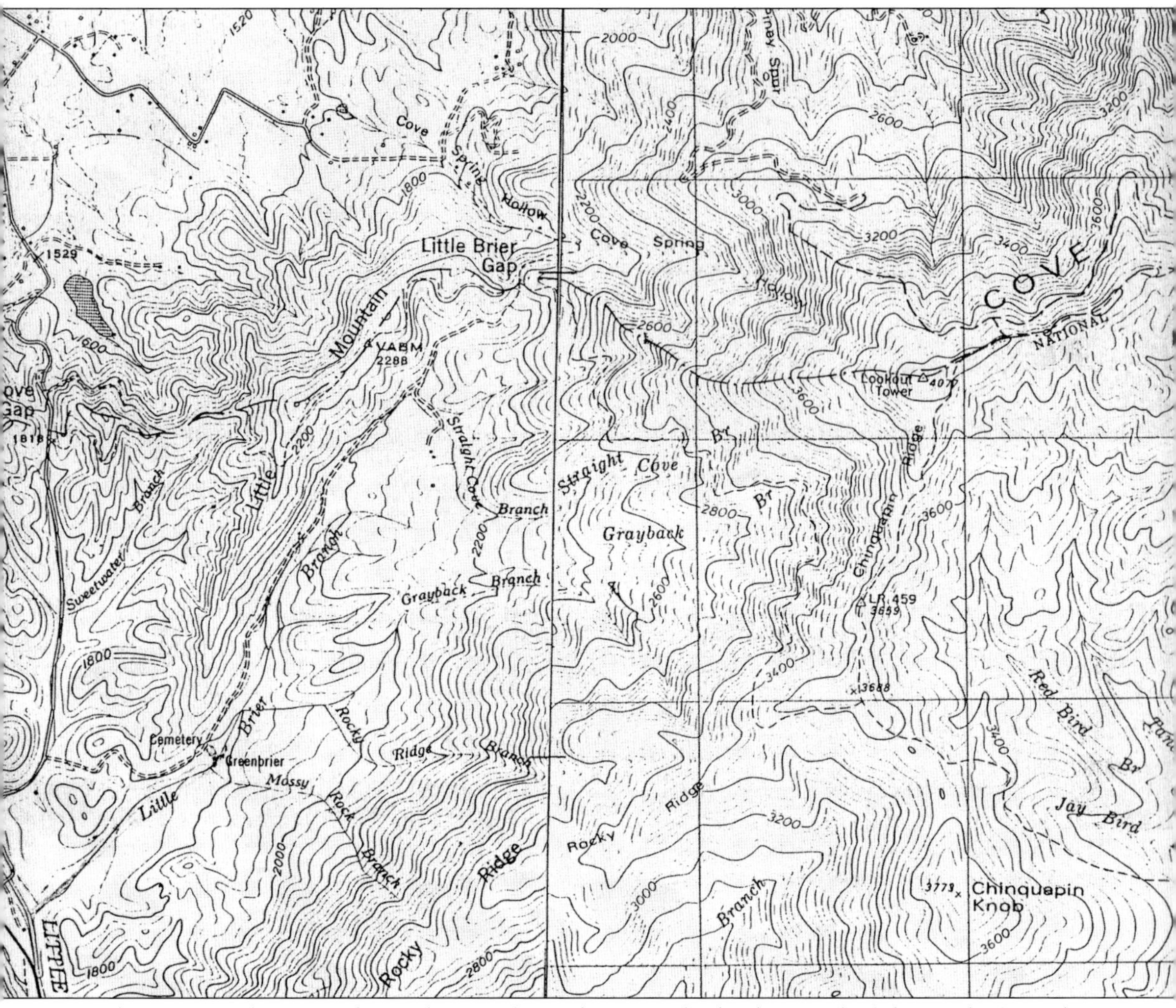

This topographic map shows that Rocky Ridge is in the background of the Little Greenbrier School, which is in a relatively flat area considering the terrain. (Courtesy Great Smoky Mountains National Park archives.)

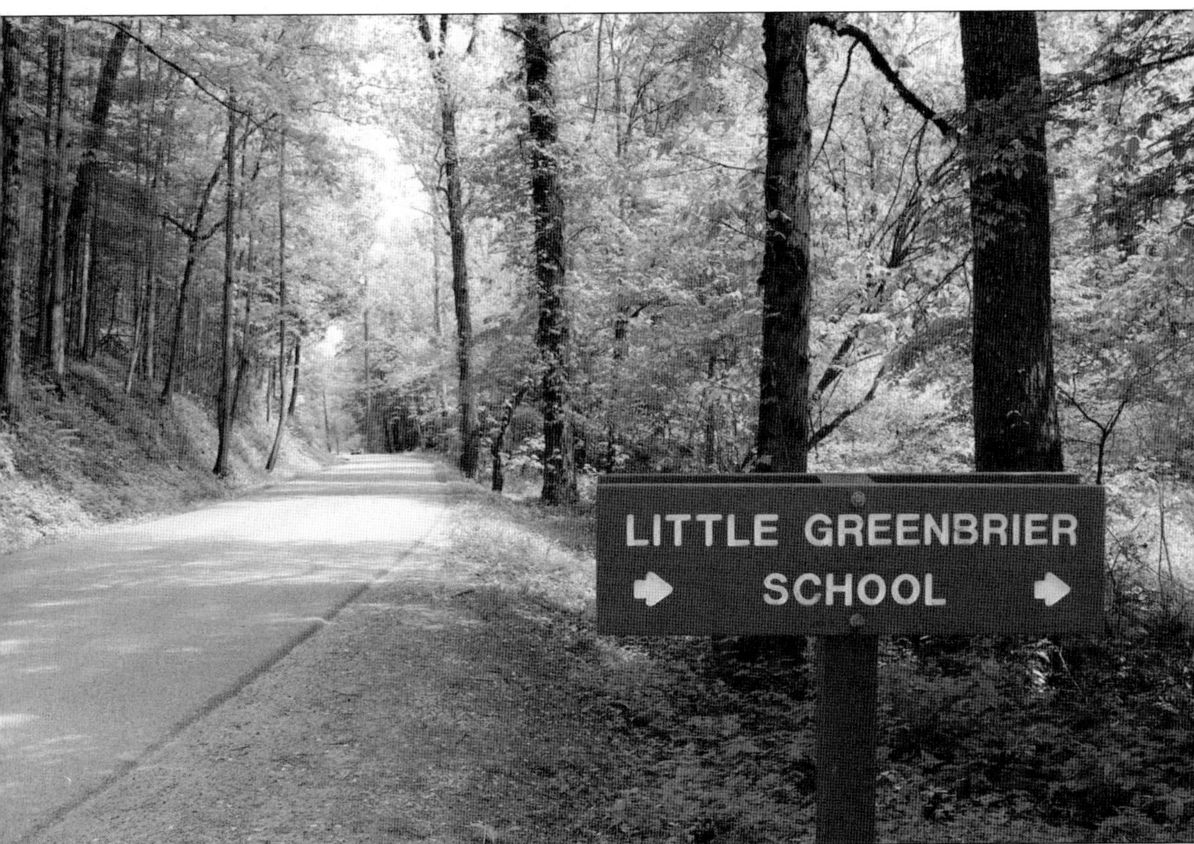

The Little Greenbrier School is off Wears Cove Road in the northern section of Great Smoky Mountains National Park. There is now a double-sided sign, so visitors can easily find the school. (Photograph by author.)

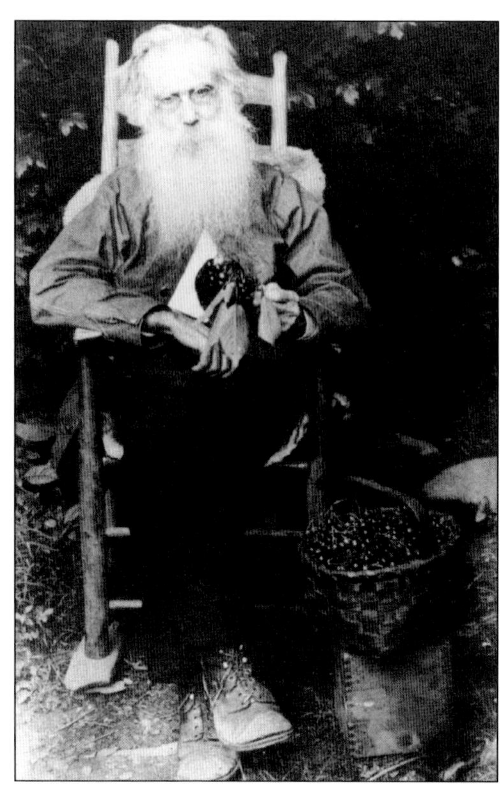

John Walker is shown with the fruits of his labor—a basket of cherries at left and apples below. Walker was known for his fondness for growing fruit and planting numerous varieties of apple trees. (Both, courtesy Great Smoky Mountains National Park archives.)

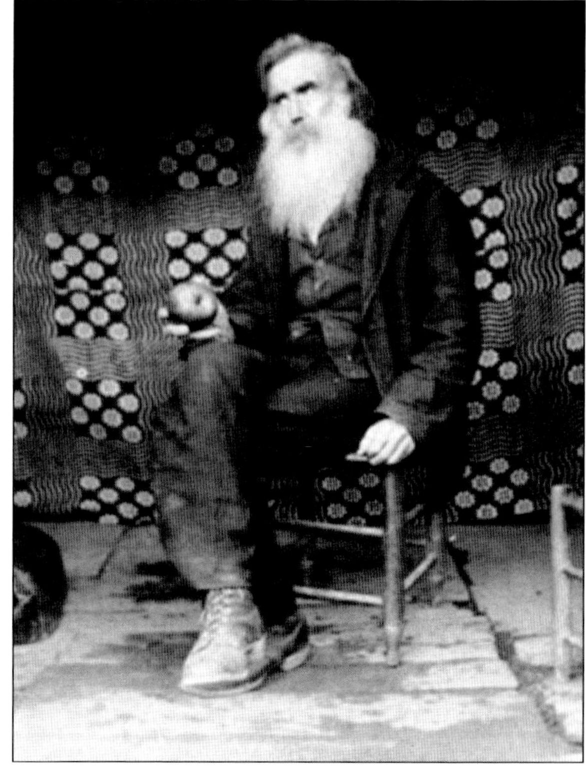

Friends Jim Shelton (left) and Lem Ownby are pictured at Ownby's home in the 1950s or 1960s. Ownby was a blind beekeeper from the Elkmont area of the park. (Courtesy Great Smoky Mountains National Park archives.)

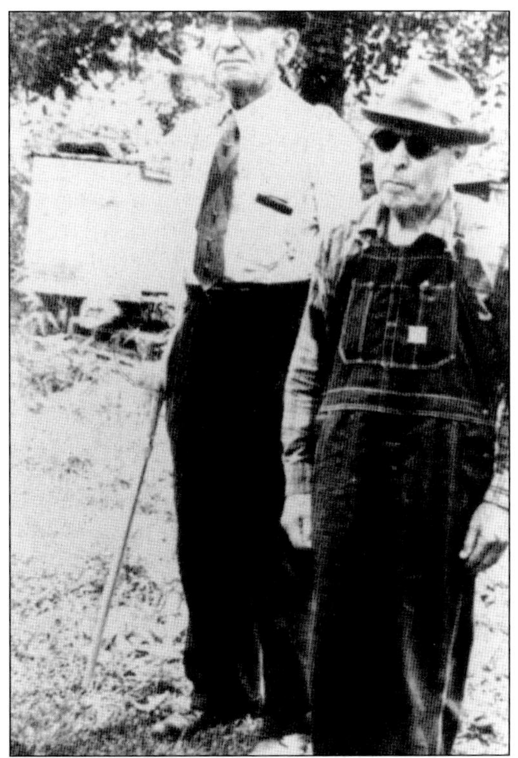

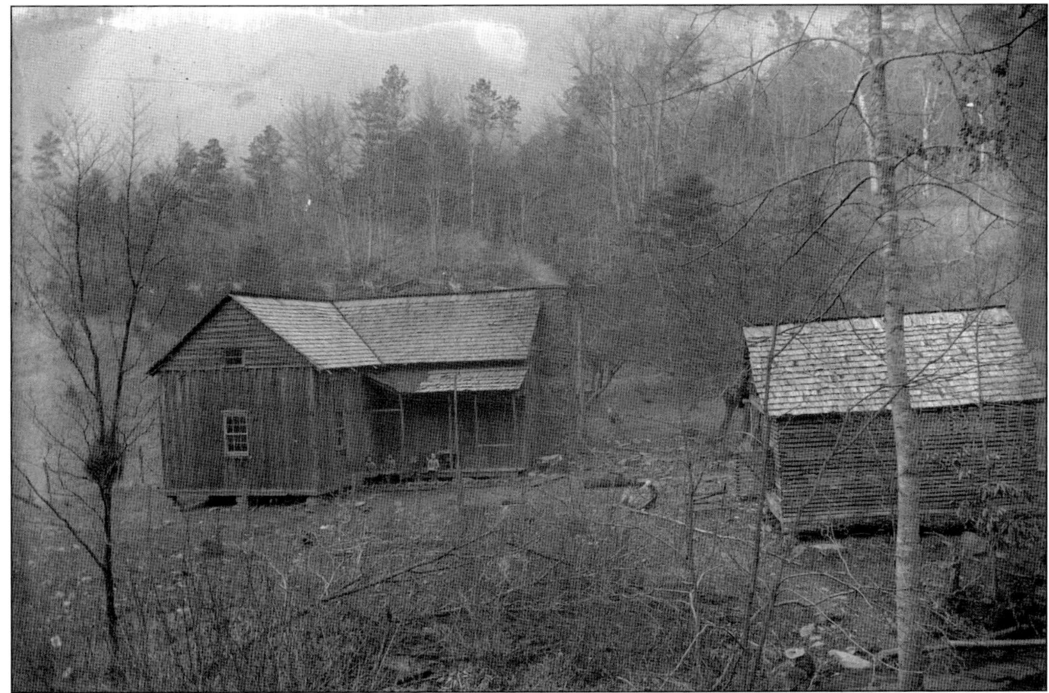

A note on the negative of this photograph reads, "Jim Shelton sold home built by him and tore down by him, circa 1914–1936, saved lumber." Shelton's home was very close to the Little Greenbrier School. (Courtesy Great Smoky Mountains National Park archives.)

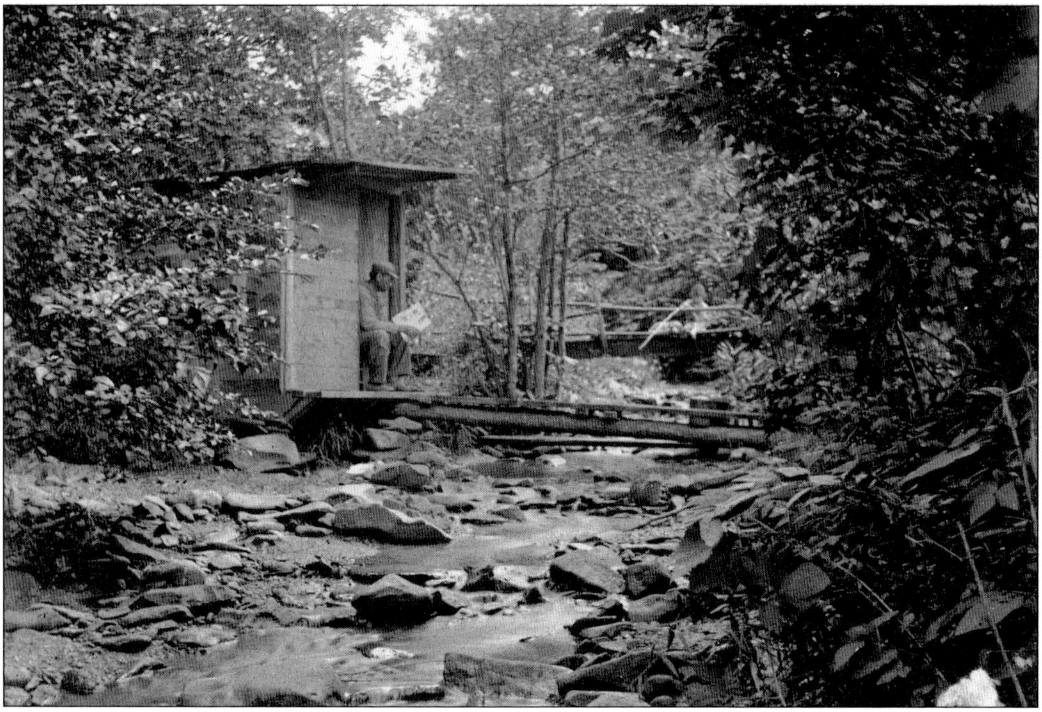

This small building was Jim Shelton's studio. Built on a stream near his home, this is where he developed his many photographs of the Little Greenbrier School and the Walker family. (Courtesy Great Smoky Mountains National Park archives.)

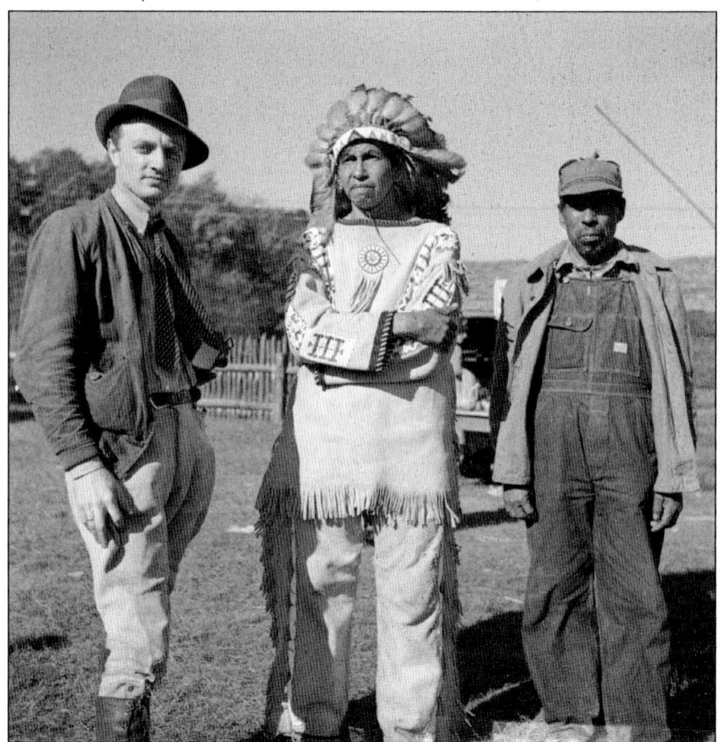

E.E. Exline, at left, poses with two Cherokee acquaintances. Exline took photographs at the Little Greenbrier School on its last day of operation in 1936. (Courtesy Great Smoky Mountains National Park archives.)

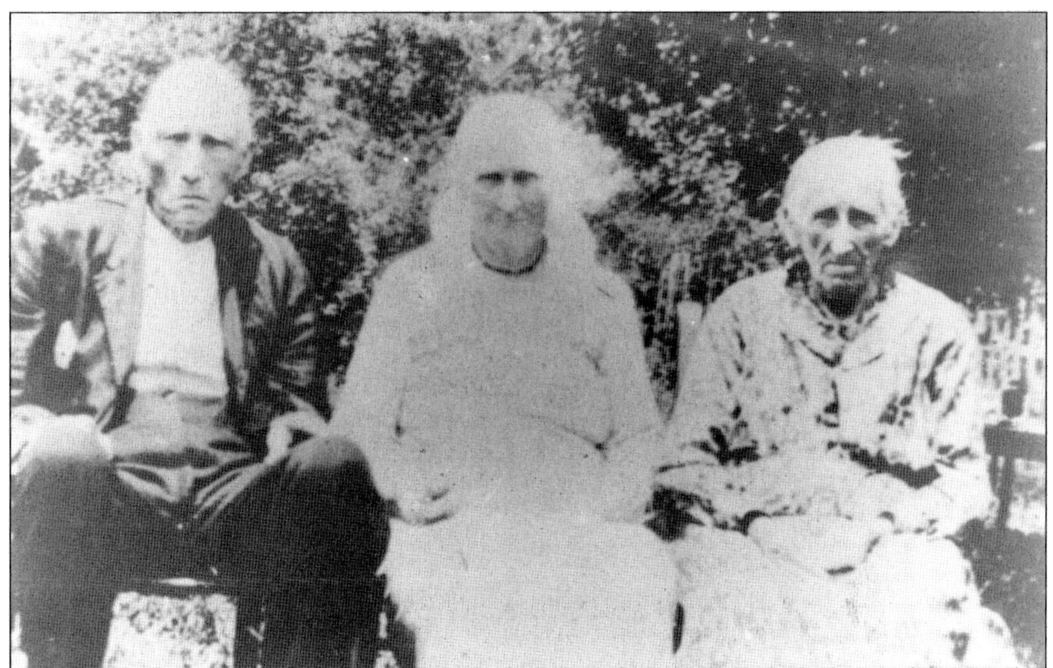

Pictured here from left to right are Ephraim Ogle, who donated the trees used for building the Little Greenbrier School, with his wife, Mary Ann Reagan Ogle, and Nancy Reagan Abbott. Ephraim Ogle passed away in 1936. (Courtesy Great Smoky Mountains National Park archives.)

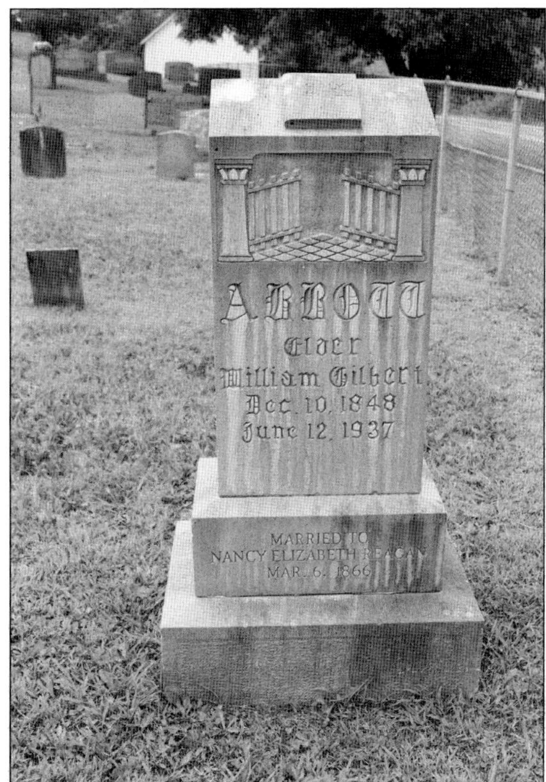

William Gilbert Abbott donated the land for the school. He was also selected to help construct the building as a cornerman. He is buried at Headrick Chapel in Wears Valley, Tennessee. (Photograph by author.)

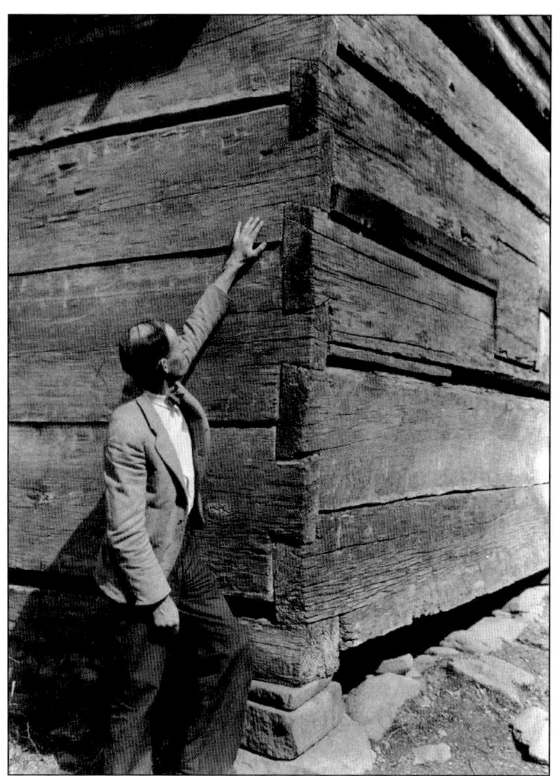

Herman Matthews, the last teacher at the Little Greenbrier School, shows the dovetail notching on the building. It was noted on this photograph that the second log from the bottom had a 28-inch face. (Courtesy Great Smoky Mountains National Park archives.)

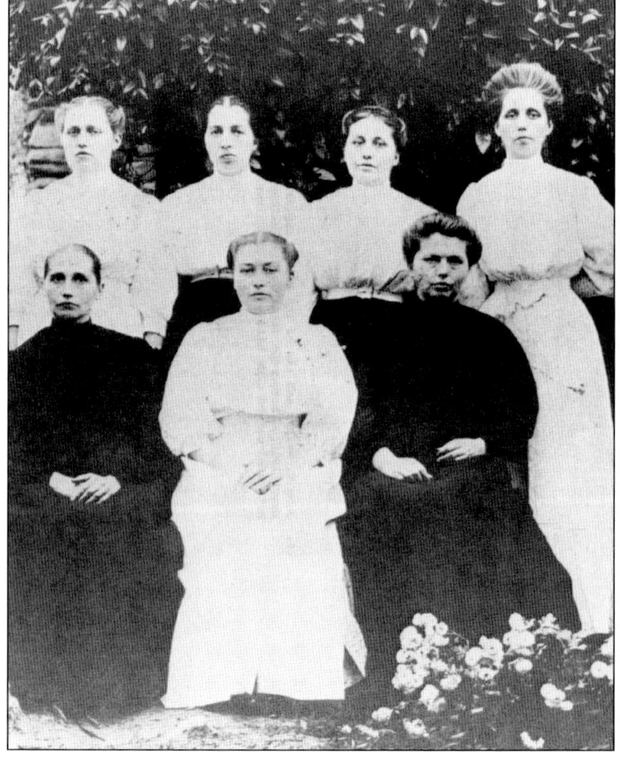

The Walker sisters are the most famous residents of the Little Greenbrier community. They lived 1.1 miles from the Little Greenbrier School, which they and their brothers attended. From left to right are (first row) Margaret, Louisa, and Polly; (second row) Hettie, Martha, Nancy, and Sarah Caroline. (Courtesy Great Smoky Mountains National Park archives.)

Two

School Days

The Little Greenbrier School ran seasonally from January 1882 to 1900, when it closed for one year. Some say the shutdown was due to a lack of funds, but others blame it on a land dispute—regarding the deed—between the donor of the land and Maj. C.D. Turner, a Civil War veteran. Major Turner took out the flooring of the school and all but two benches. One original bench remains at the school today, and the other is in the national park headquarters in Gatlinburg, Tennessee. Naturally, the community was upset over the loss of the building, and asked Sevier County to buy the building and provide a teacher. Fifty dollars bought two acres and the building, and provided a teacher's salary for the season. School resumed in the building in 1901 and remained there until the 1935–1936 term, after which it closed for good.

There were 41 teachers at the Little Greenbrier School. In *Upland Chronicles of the Smokies*, Carroll McMahan writes, "The second teacher at Little Greenbrier was James B. Lawson of Wear's Valley [*sic*]. Known as One-Armed Jimmy, Lawson had his paralyzed arm cut off when he was a young man. After teaching at Little Greenbrier, stories about the former teacher fascinated the students. He was a linguist, athlete, prospector, amateur astronomer, world traveler, and genealogist."

It is doubtful the other teachers were as interesting as Mr. Lawson.

According to a HABS report,

> Enrollment rose steadily, to a peak of 73 pupils in 1923. In 1924-25 Little River Lumber company pulled its railroad tracks from Little River gorge, and moved its operation to Tremont. This caused an immediate drop of 35-40%, as the kids' families moved to the new logging site. A second blow followed in the late 1920s and early 30s, as the park land acquisition program got underway and more people moved out of the cove. In the last school term (1935-36) there were only 25 pupils left. . . . The school property was purchased from the Sevier County Board of Education, August 26, 1933, by the Tennessee Park Commission while acquiring lands to form the Great Smoky Mountains National Park.

In March 1936, during the last month in which classes were held, photographer E.E. Exline came to the school. Luckily for future generations, he took many pictures that day, which have been preserved for posterity.

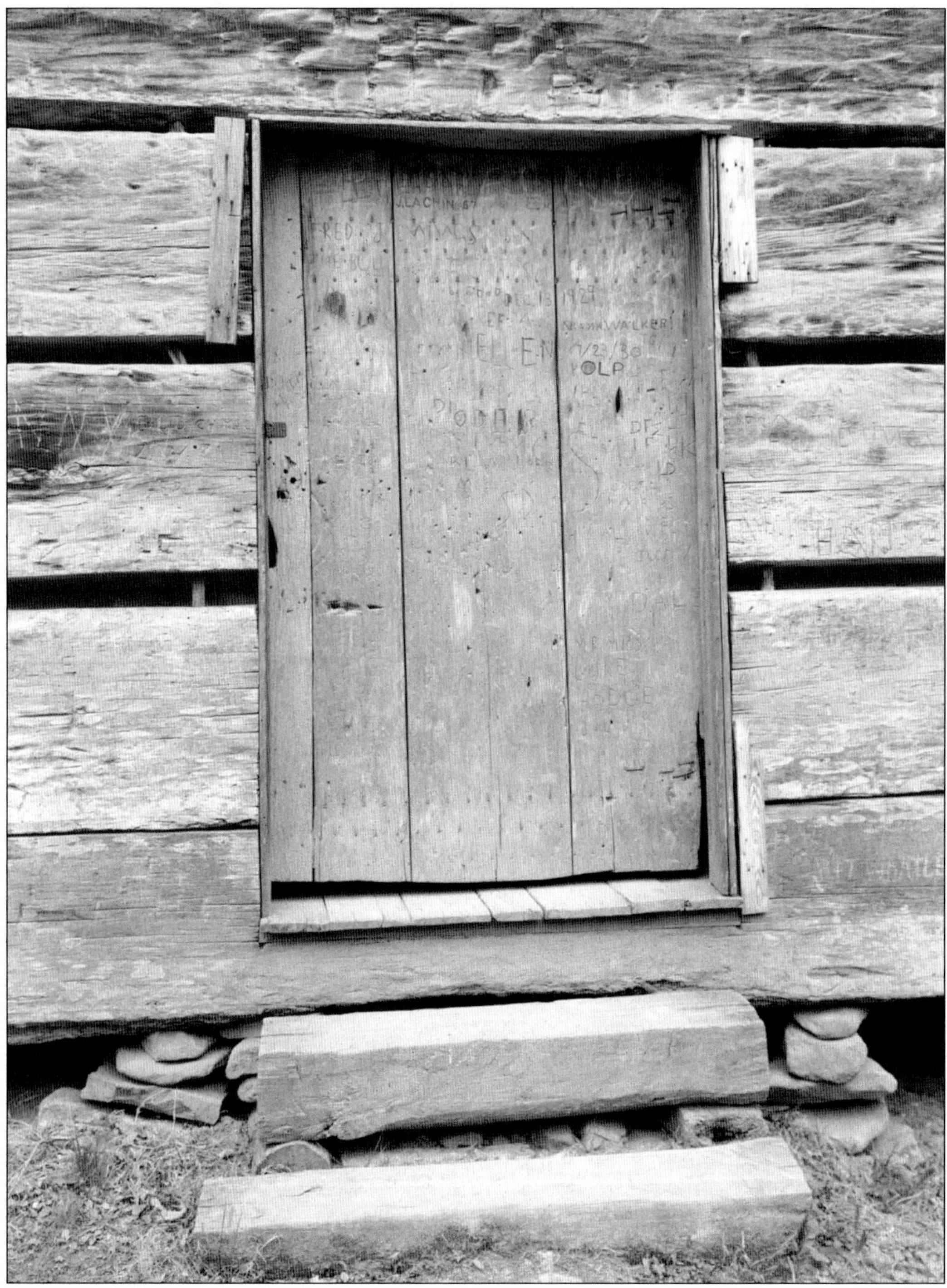

Thousands of people have entered the Little Greenbrier School through this one and only door, but none were as important as the students who actually attended school here. Note the dogwood tree supports next to the door. (Courtesy Great Smoky Mountains National Park archives.)

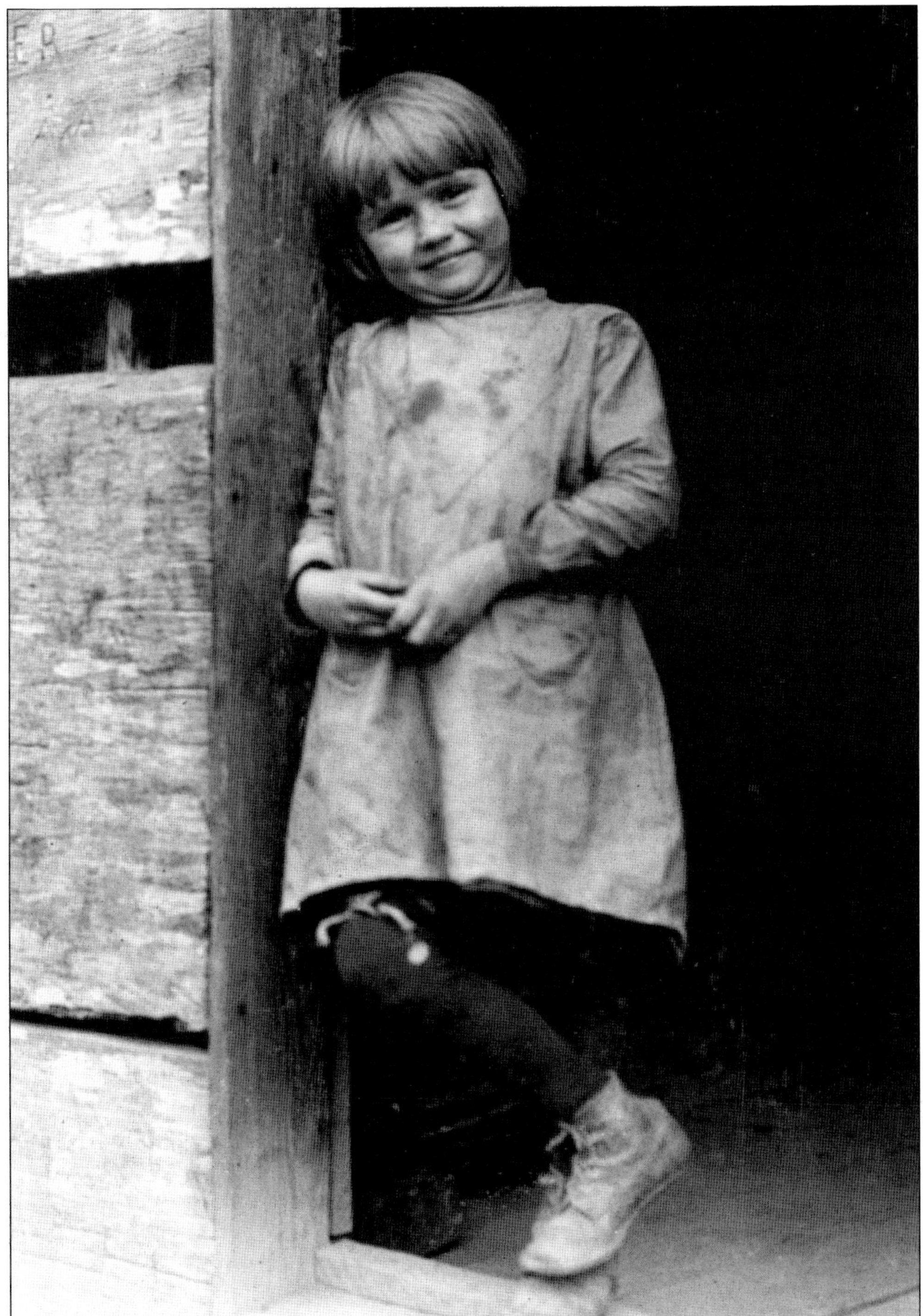

Class pictures were popular, even in older schools. Several such images are included in this book. The only identification on this photograph refers to the subject as a "Mountain Child" at the Little Greenbrier School. It is dated March 1935 and was taken by Donald Wolbrink. (Courtesy Great Smoky Mountains National Park archives.)

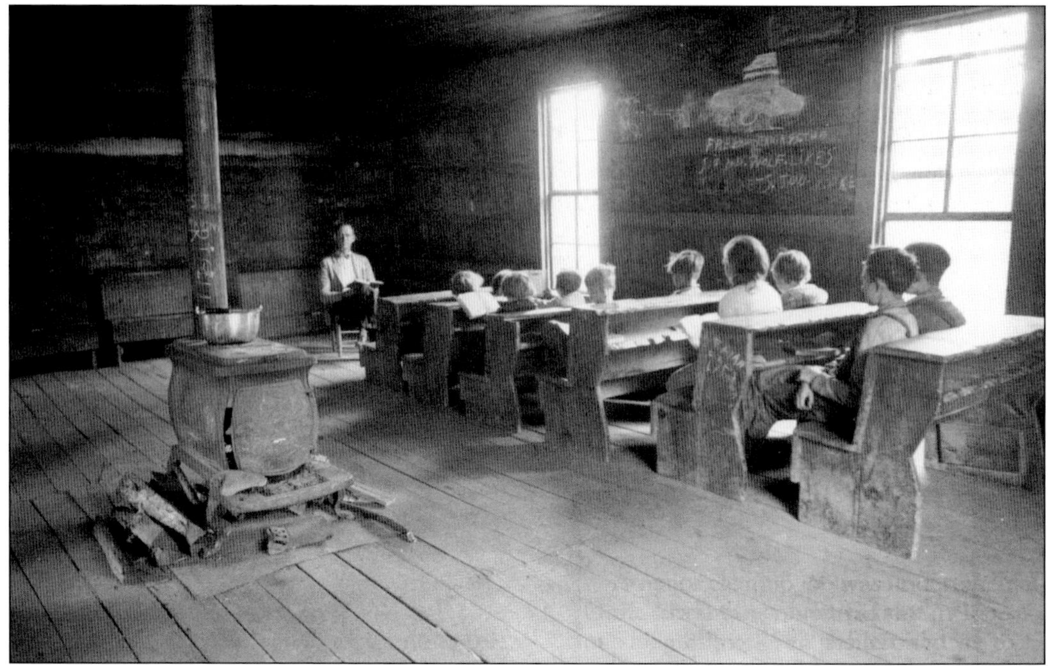

The stove for the school was in the middle of the room and provided warmth for the entire building. It was removed when vandals tried to dismantle it for souvenirs. Herman Matthews, pictured here, taught on the last day the school was in operation. The third set of benches, with a seat, shelf for writing, and cubby hole for books, are still in use as of this writing. (Courtesy Great Smoky Mountains National Park archives.)

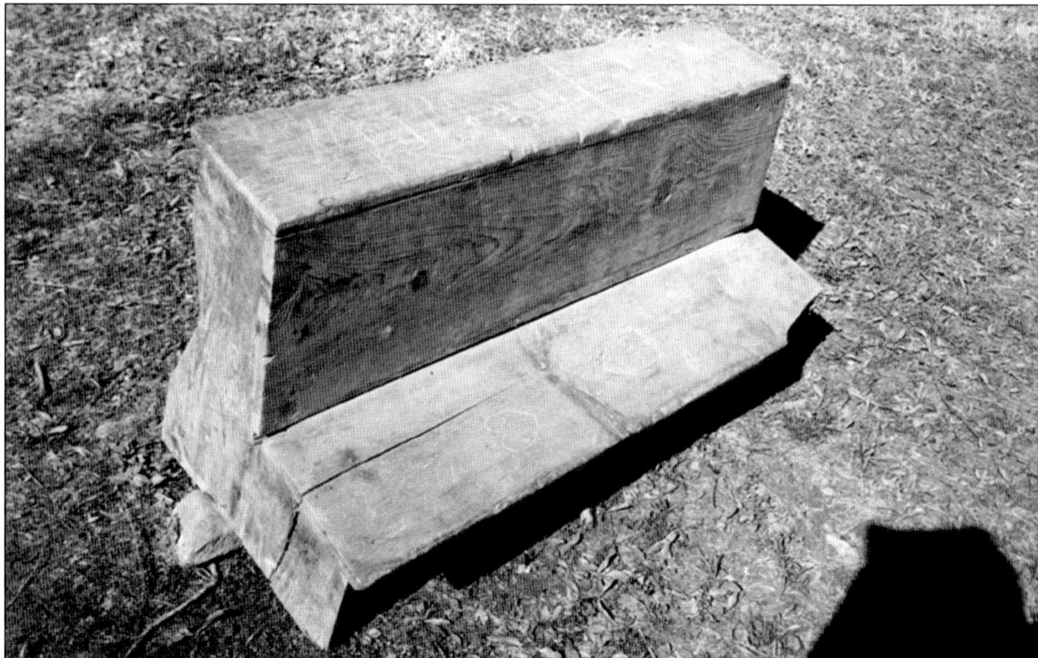

This is one of the benches used later in the school's life. At the time it was photographed, there was little to no graffiti on it. (Courtesy Great Smoky Mountains National Park archives.)

Student Conley Russell seemed to enjoy having his picture taken on March 2, 1936. Russell passed away on March 12, 1997, and is buried in the Valley View Cemetery in Wears Valley. (Courtesy Great Smoky Mountains National Park archives.)

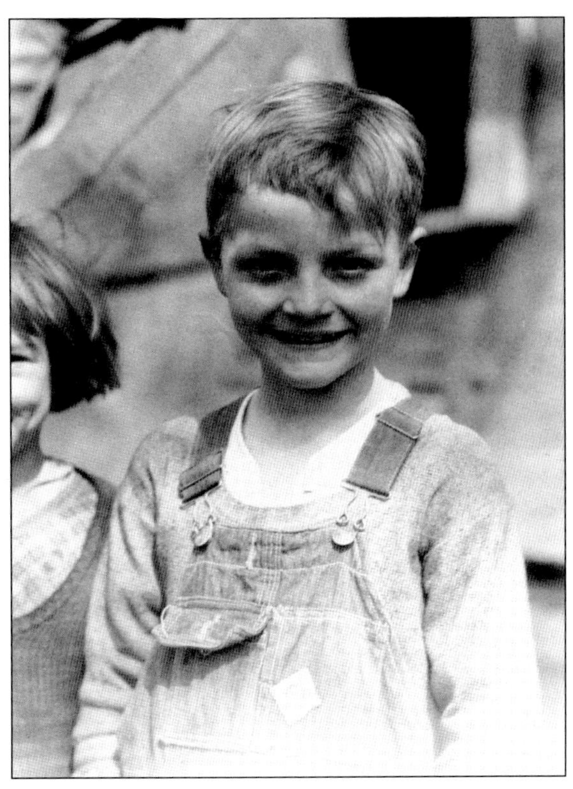

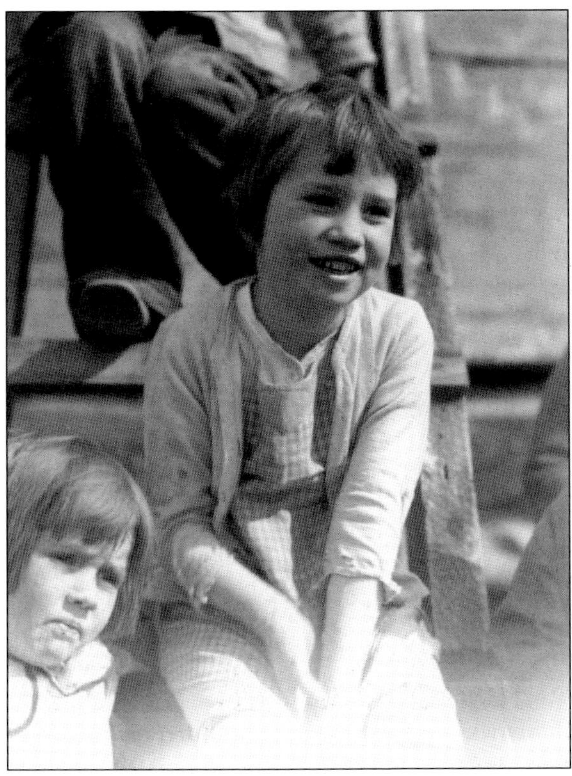

Rowena Tallent is smiling in this photograph by E.E. Exline taken on the last day of school in 1936. Tallent passed away on May 30, 1998. (Courtesy Great Smoky Mountains National Park archives.)

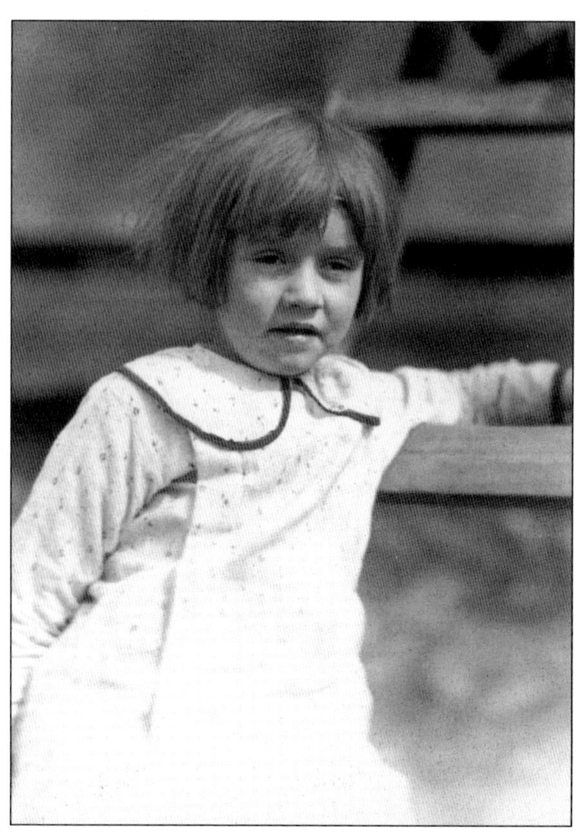

Mary Moore also posed for Exline on the last day of school. She is leaning on the ladder that was used to recaulk the chimney and access the attic. (Courtesy Great Smoky Mountains National Park archives.)

Betty Moore, one of a handful of children left at the Little Greenbrier School, spent her last day at the school with friends. She is shown in this photograph by E.E. Exline. Moore visited the school in the early 2000s to go down memory lane, and passed away the next day. (Courtesy Great Smoky Mountains National Park archives.)

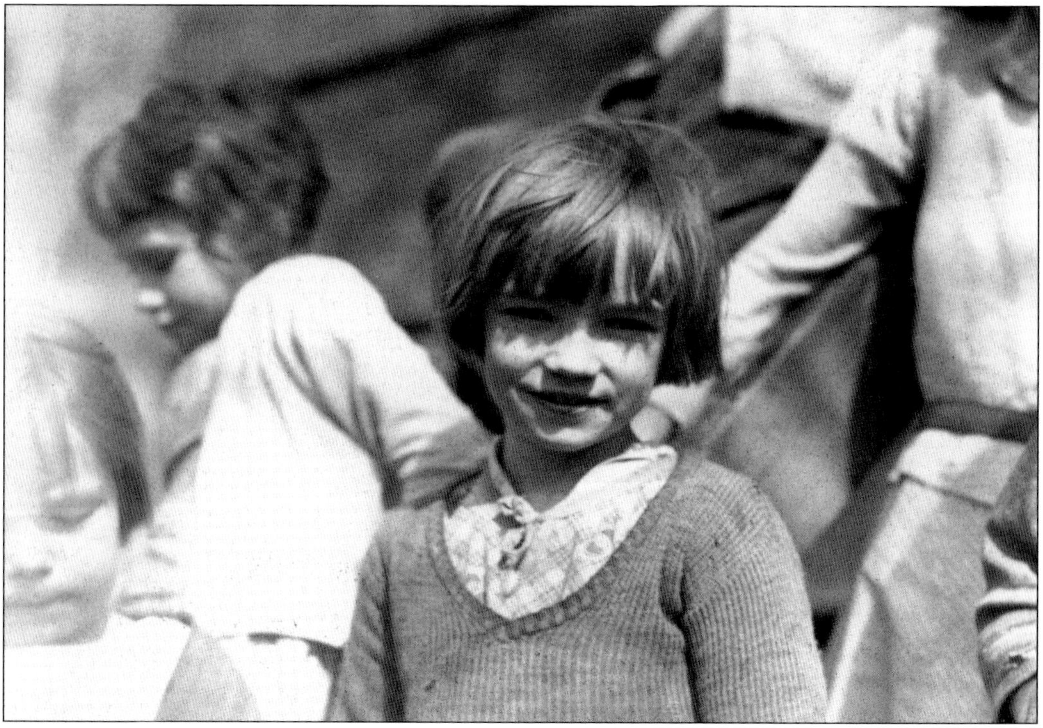

Margaret "Billy" Tallent was seemingly shy in this Exline picture from March 2, 1936, her last day of school. (Courtesy Great Smoky Mountains National Park archives.)

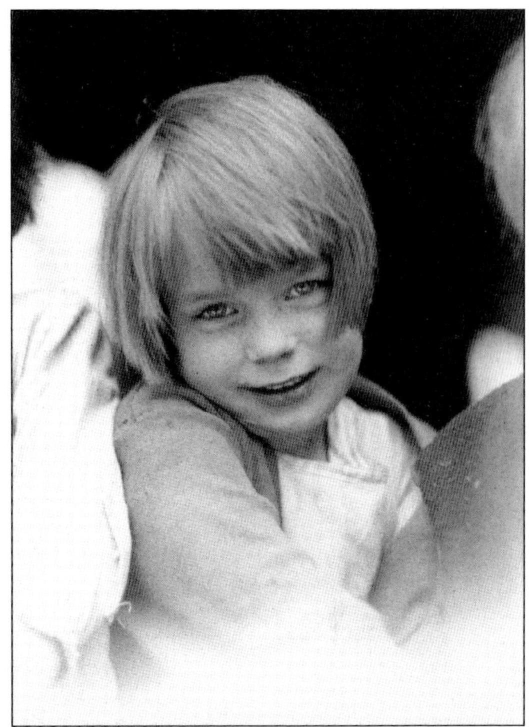

Up until 2021, there were 27 benches in the school, including a double row on the left side, with two benches touching, and a double row on the right with an aisle down the middle. Vandals destroyed one bench during the COVID-19 pandemic. (Courtesy Friends of the Smokies.)

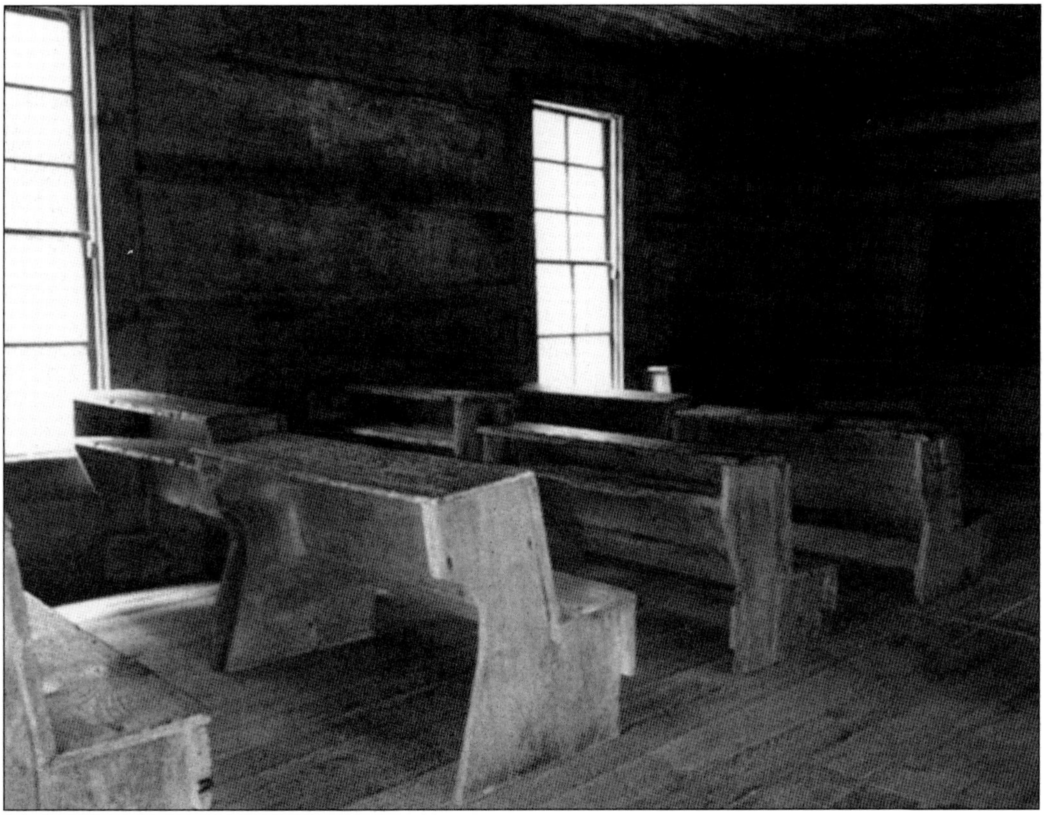

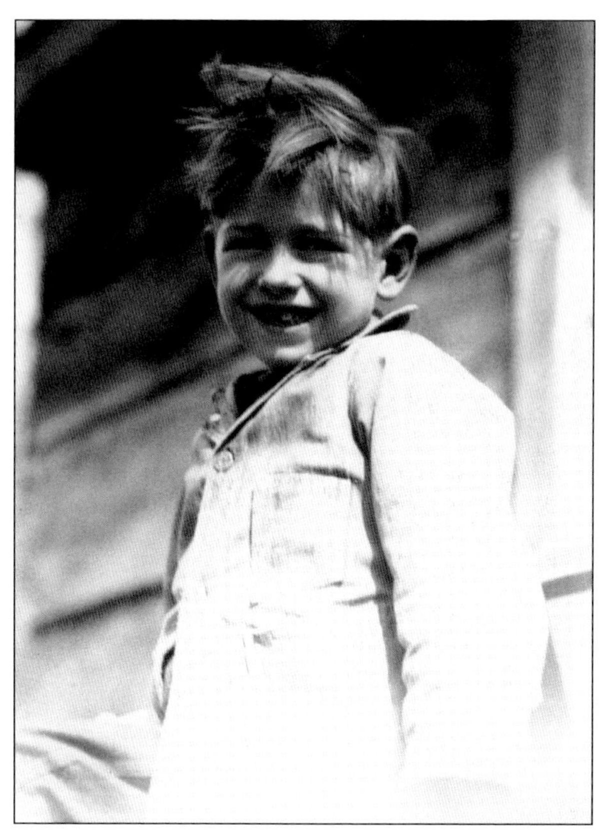

Student Harold Walker, the youngest son of James Thomas Walker, enjoyed the attention of photographer E.E. Exline in 1936. Below, he is pictured as an adult with Robin Goddard at the Little Greenbrier School. He passed away on June 21, 2012. (Left, courtesy Great Smoky Mountains National Park archives; below, courtesy Robin Goddard.)

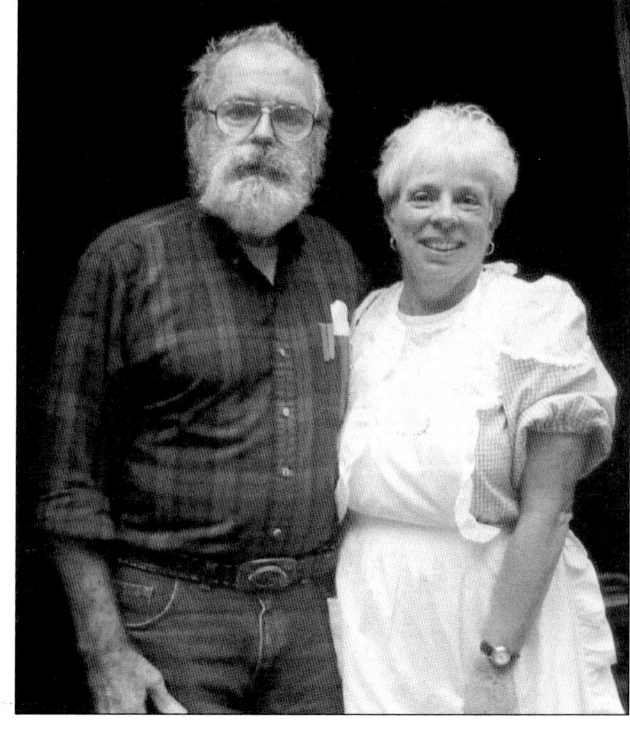

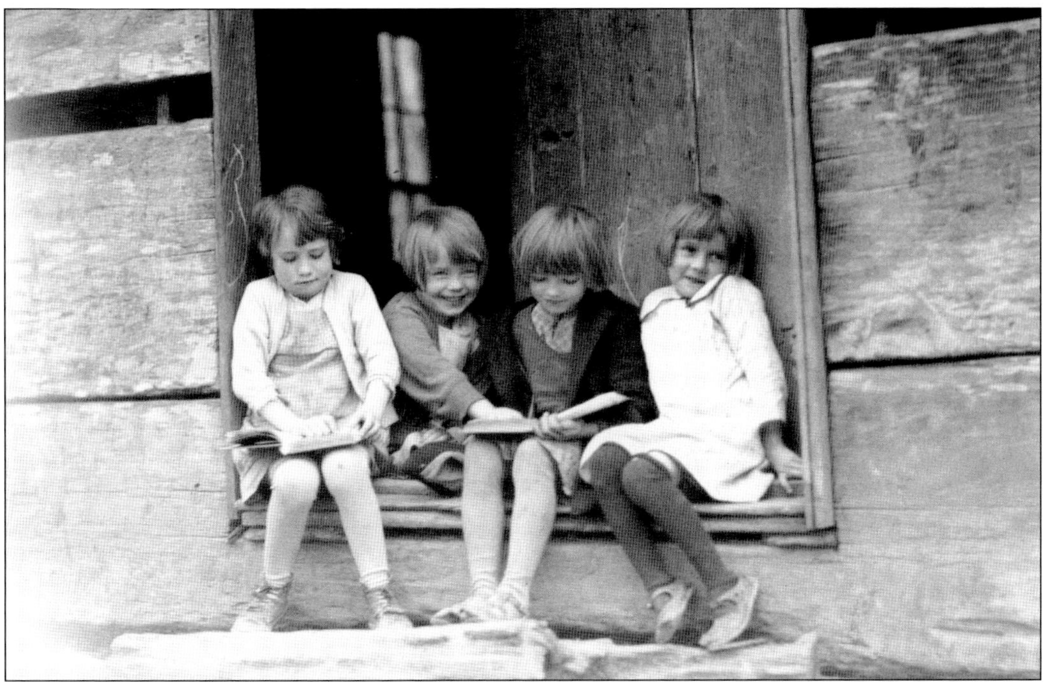

Rowena Tallent, Margaret (Billy) Tallent, Betty Moore, and Mary Moore were photographed by E.E. Exline at the Little Greenbrier School. This was probably the last day they were all together before their families moved away from the cove. (Courtesy Great Smoky Mountains National Park archives.)

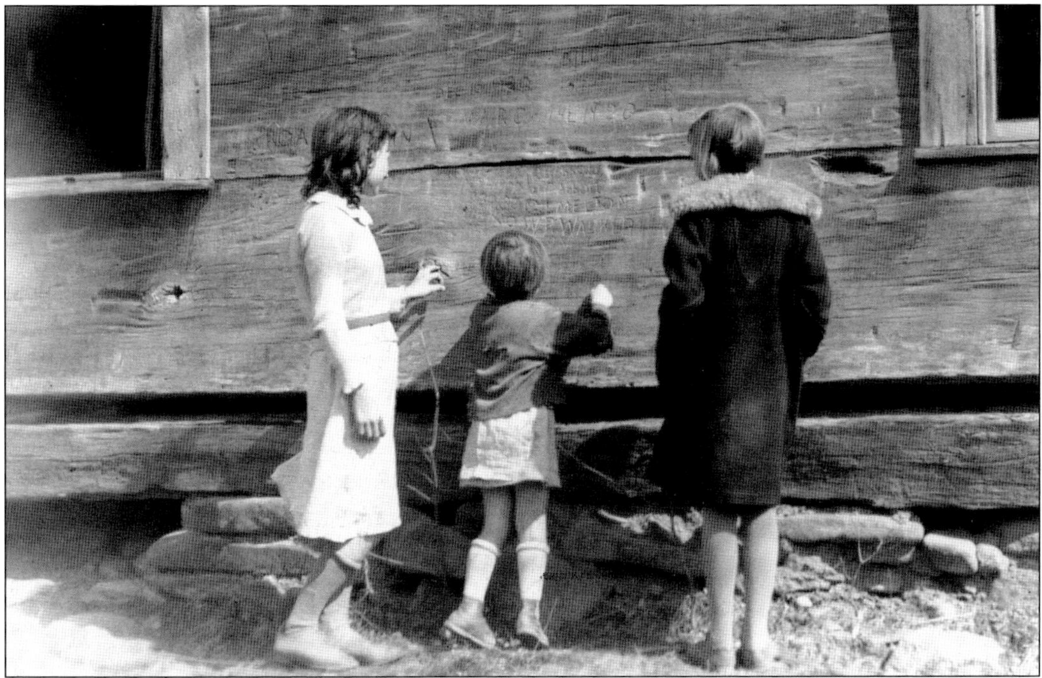

Helen Moore, Margaret Tallent, and Edith Moore are examining the outside of the school on March 2, 1936. (Courtesy Great Smoky Mountains National Park archives.)

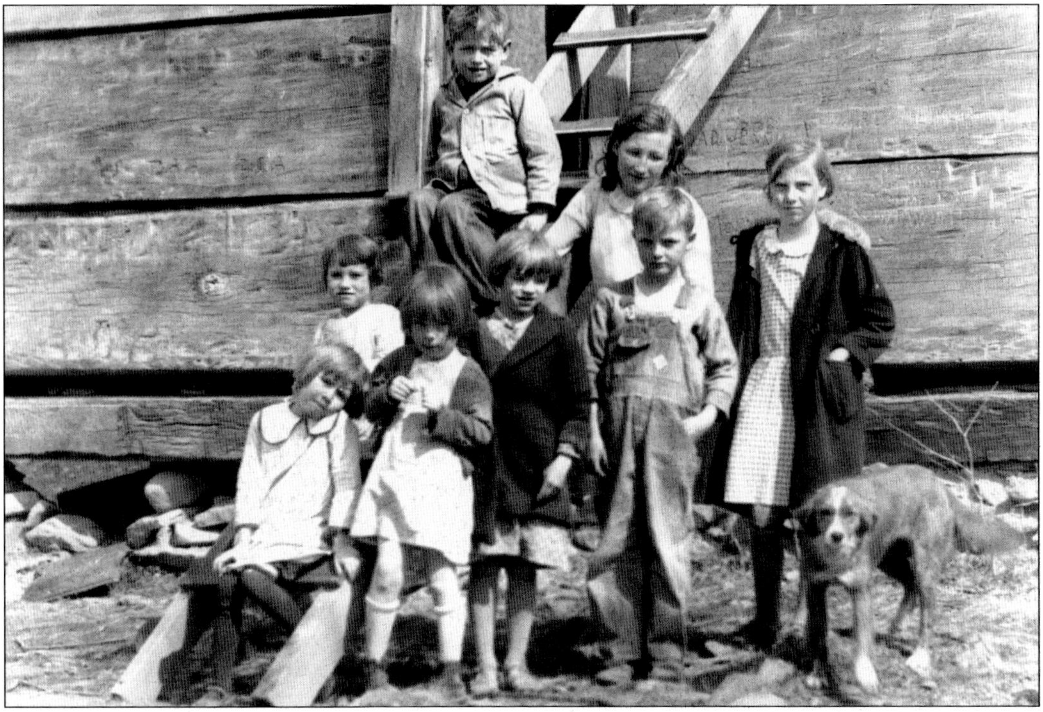

This photograph of part of the class of 1936 outside the Little Greenbrier School shows that someone's dog was allowed to go to school that day. (Courtesy Great Smoky Mountains National Park archives.)

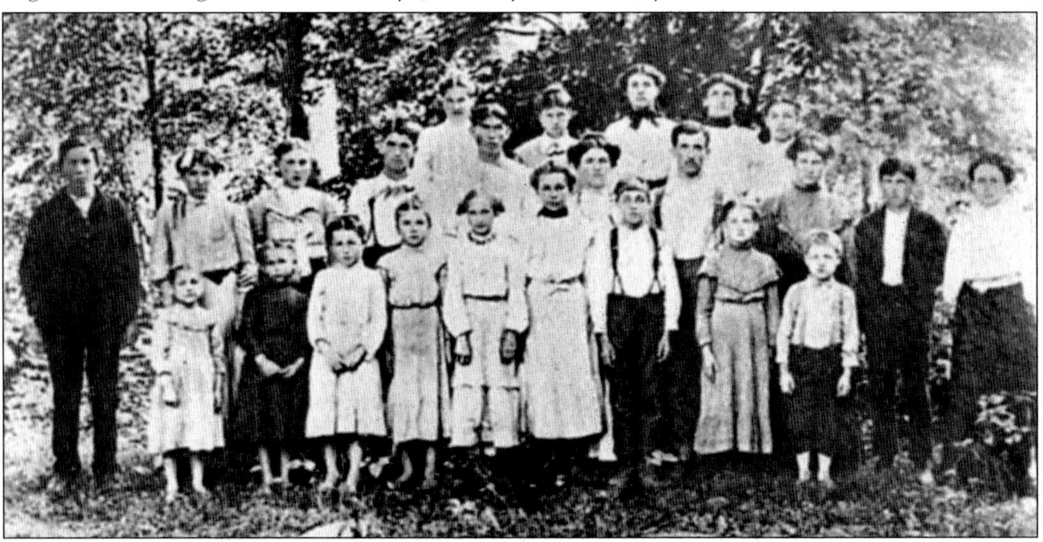

This is the 1906 Little Greenbrier School picture taken by Jim Shelton. From left to right are (first row) unidentified, Liz Kirkland, Rose Kirkland, unidentified, May Moore, Hattie Kirkland, Bob Stinnett, Hettie Stinnett, and Dan Stinnett; (second row) unidentified, Mary Moore, Cassie Moore, John Stinnett, James Stinnett, Lou Stinnett, Manning Stinnett, Cassie Moore, John Stinnett, and teacher Ana Ogle; (third row) Matt Moore, Annie Stinnett, two unidentified, and Jane Kirkland. Note that Cassie Moore and John Stinnett were mentioned twice. This image is from the pamphlet "Rememberin' The Little Greenbriar School and Primitive Baptist Church," by Margaret Stinnett Crabtree. (Courtesy Robin Goddard.)

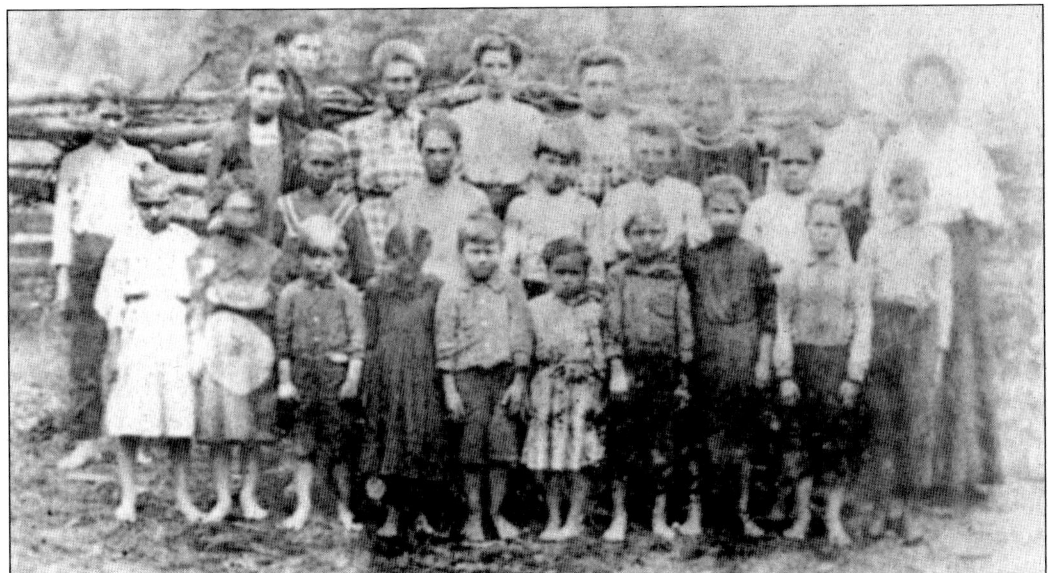

This is the 1907 school picture taken by Jim Shelton. Pictured are, presumably from left to right, (first row) two unidentified, George Walker, two unidentified, Lena Walker, Ernest Walker, unidentified, and John Stinnett; (second row) Reuben Stinnett, Lizzie Kirkland, Emma Stinnett, Dan Stinnett, Rose Kirkland, Mary Jane Walker, and Oliver Lawson; (third row) John Henry Abbott, Hattie Kirkland, Cassie Moore, Jane Kirkland, Mae Moore, Hettie Walker, and teacher Malinda King; (fourth row) Dan Walker. This image is also from "Rememberin' The Little Greenbriar School and Primitive Baptist Church." (Courtesy Robin Goddard.)

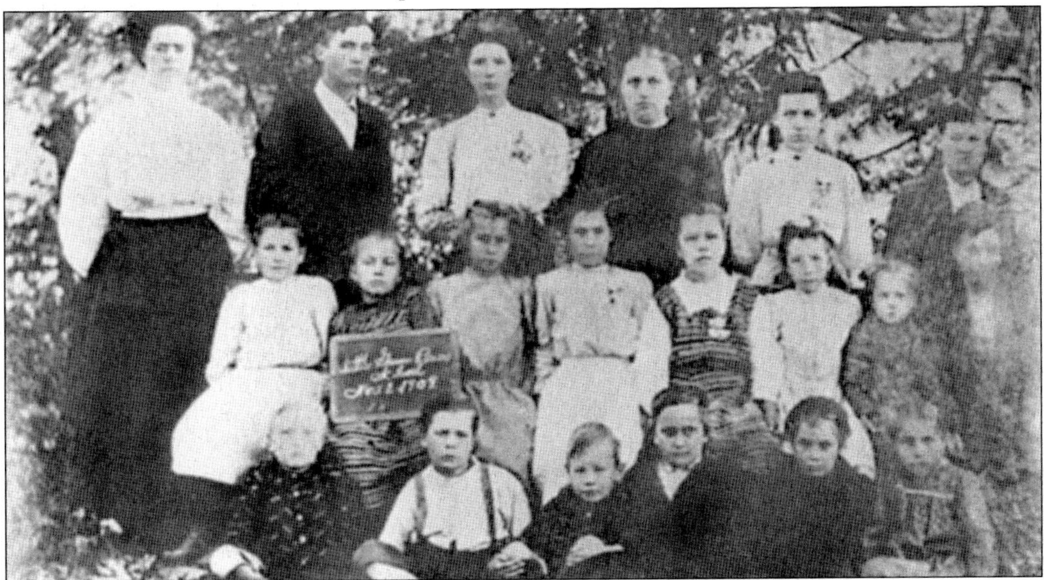

This school picture was taken on November 1, 1909. Presumably from left to right are (first row) Ernest Walker, Johnny Stinnett, George Walker, Oliver Lawson, Mary Stinnett, and Nora Walker; (second row) Ida Stinnett, Alice Walker, Lizzie Kirkland, Emma Stinnett, Mary Walker, Maude Kirkland, Lena Walker, and Reuben Stinnett; (third row) teacher Malinda King, Dan Walker, Cassie Moore, Hettie Walker, Ellen Walker, and John Abbott. (Courtesy Great Smoky Mountains National Park archives.)

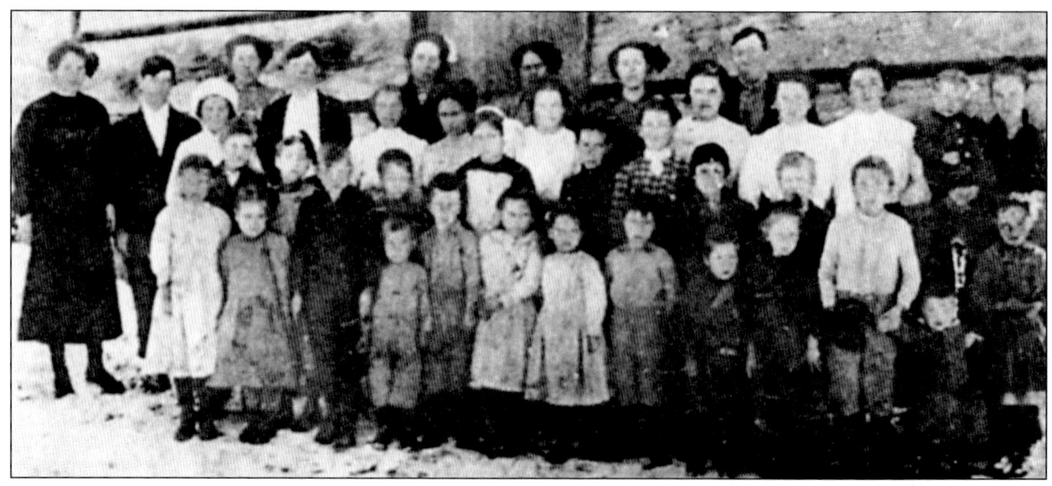

This is the 1912 school picture taken by Jim Shelton. Presumably from left to right are (first row) Blan Shelton, Mamie Walker, Alex Moore, Frank Kirkland, Sam Kirkland, Rose Shelton, Nora Shelton, Walter Kirkland, Frank Walker, Evelyn Walker, Will Kirkland, Ethel Kirkland, and Laura Moore; (second row) Ernest Walker, Nora Walker, Lena Walker, Alice Walker, Rose Kirkland, Ida Stinnett, Charlie Parton, and George Walker; (third row) Willie Wear, Fate Green, Lizzie Kirkland, Alice Shelton, Rebecca Green, Mary Walker, Maude Kirkland, Jane Kirkland, Nancy Stinnett, and Mary Alice Moore; (fourth row) Annie King, Abbott Warwick, Johnny Abbott, Alice King, Myrtle King, Jane King, teacher Malinda King, and John Kirkland. This is from "Rememberin' The Little Greenbriar School and Primitive Baptist Church." (Courtesy Robin Goddard.)

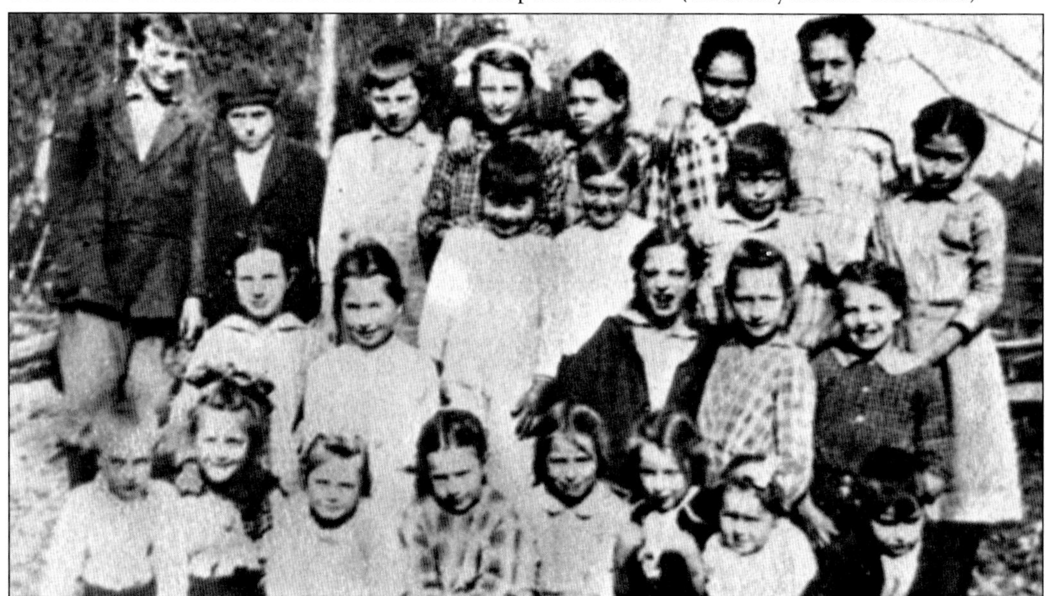

This is the 1916 school picture by Jim Shelton. Presumably from left to right are (first row) John Moore, Stella Moore, Lou Moore, Mary Moore, Lucy Walker, Pearl Walker, Josie Walker, and Mell Ownby; (second row) Laurie Moore, Josie Stinnett, Ethel Walker, Evelyn Walker, and Minnie Walker; (third row) Sheryl Ownby, Roy Ownby, Frank Walker, and Mamie Walker; (fourth row) George Walker, Joe Abbott, Alex Moore, Willie Moore, Blan Shelton, Lena Walker, and Willie Abbott. The image is from "Rememberin' The Little Greenbriar School and Primitive Baptist Church." (Courtesy Robin Goddard.)

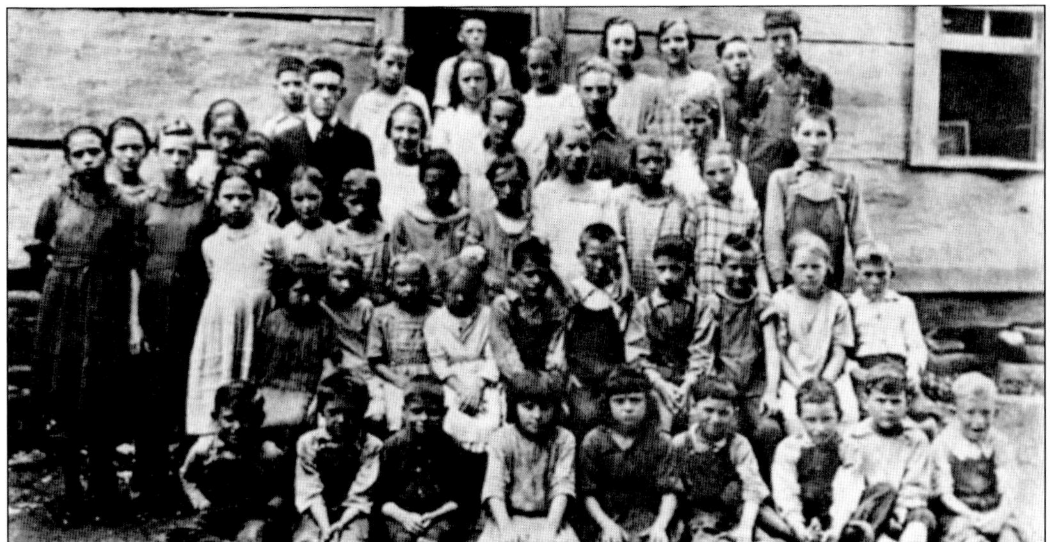

This is the 1922 school picture taken by Jim Shelton. Pictured are, presumably from left to right, (first row) John Shelton, Ernest Moore, Bill Walker, Elizabeth Wakefield, Vertie Huskey, Otis Shelton, Jim Metcalf, Jack Rhea, and Edmon Kirkland; (second row) Margery Walker, Myrtle Walker, Pearl Walker, Clementine Melton, Tom Walker, Harvey McCarter, Luther Walker, Fred Walker, Josie Walker, and Frank Cole; (third row) Hazel Shelton, Tine Huskey, Georgie Moore, Tine Metcalf, Ruth Wakefield, Lucy Walker, Etta Huskey, Mary Moore, and George Melton; (fourth row) Effie Shelton, Leona Shelton, and Rose Metcalf; (fifth row) Evelyn Walker, Mamie Walker, teacher Walter Ogle, Minnie Walker, Edith Davis, George Walker, and Ola Abbott; (sixth row) Louis Walker, Pearl Walker, Iva Rhea, Iva Davis, Nancy McCarter, Ethel Walker, Carl Melton, and Jess Huskey. Frank Walker is in the window. This image is from "Rememberin' The Little Greenbriar School and Primitive Baptist Church." (Courtesy Robin Goddard.)

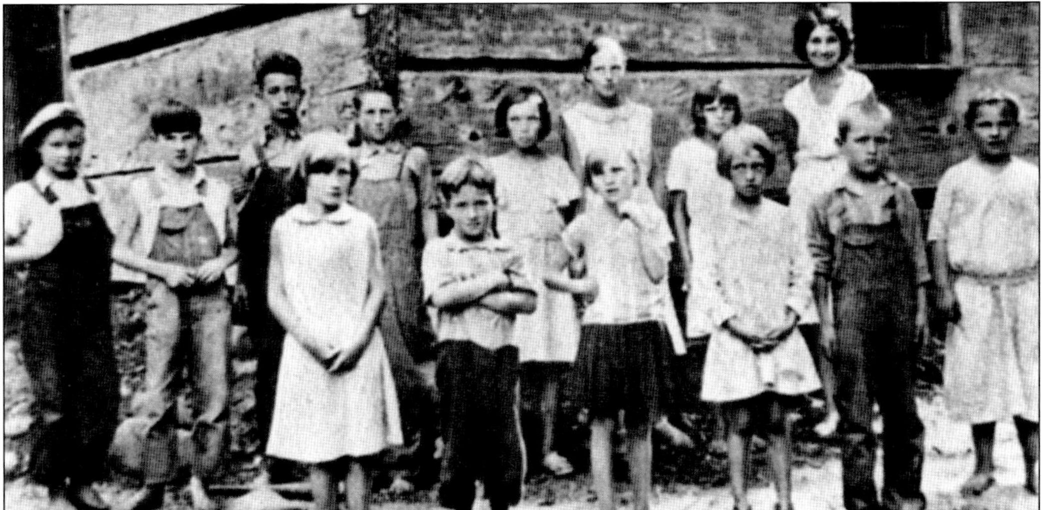

This is the 1932 school picture taken by Jim Shelton. Pictured, presumably from left to right, are (first row) Helen Moore, Louie Godfrey, Estelle Moore, Ruth Maples, "Bates" Cook, and Janie Jennings; (second row) Ray Jennings, John Moore, Robert Walker, Elmer Godfrey, Ellen Cook, Ina Walker, unidentified, and teacher Alma Headrick. This image is from "Rememberin' The Little Greenbriar School and Primitive Baptist Church." (Courtesy Robin Goddard.)

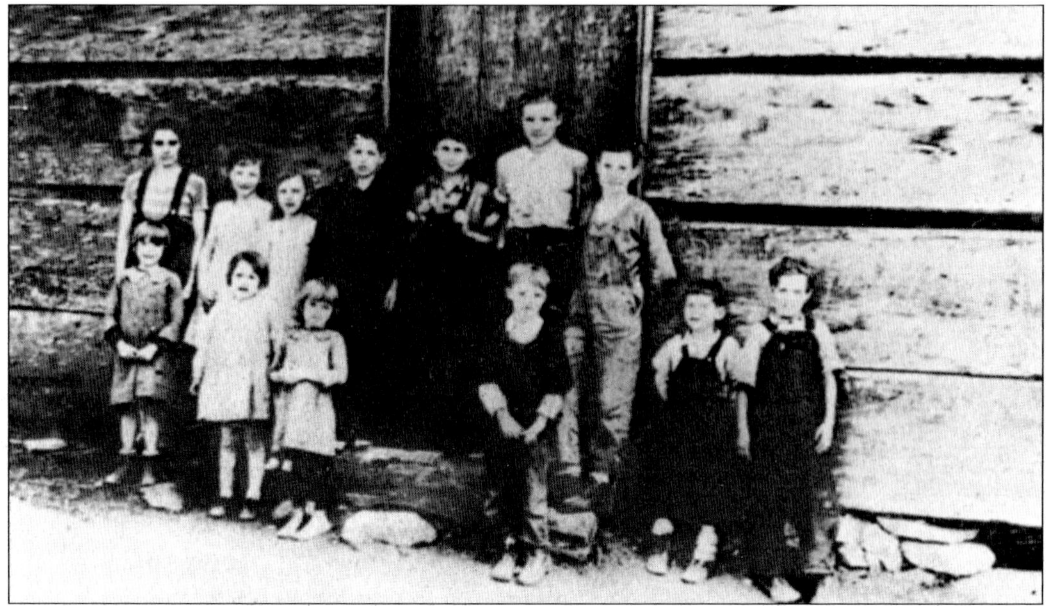

This is the 1934 school picture taken by Jim Shelton. Presumably from left to right are (first row) Betty Moore, Rowena Tallent, Mary Moore, Conley Russell, Harold Walker, and Allen Abbott; (second row) teacher Myrtle Brewer, Helen Moore, Estelle Moore, J.D. Abbott, Richard Walker, Ray Jennings, and John Moore. The image is from "Rememberin' The Little Greenbriar School and Primitive Baptist Church." (Courtesy Robin Goddard.)

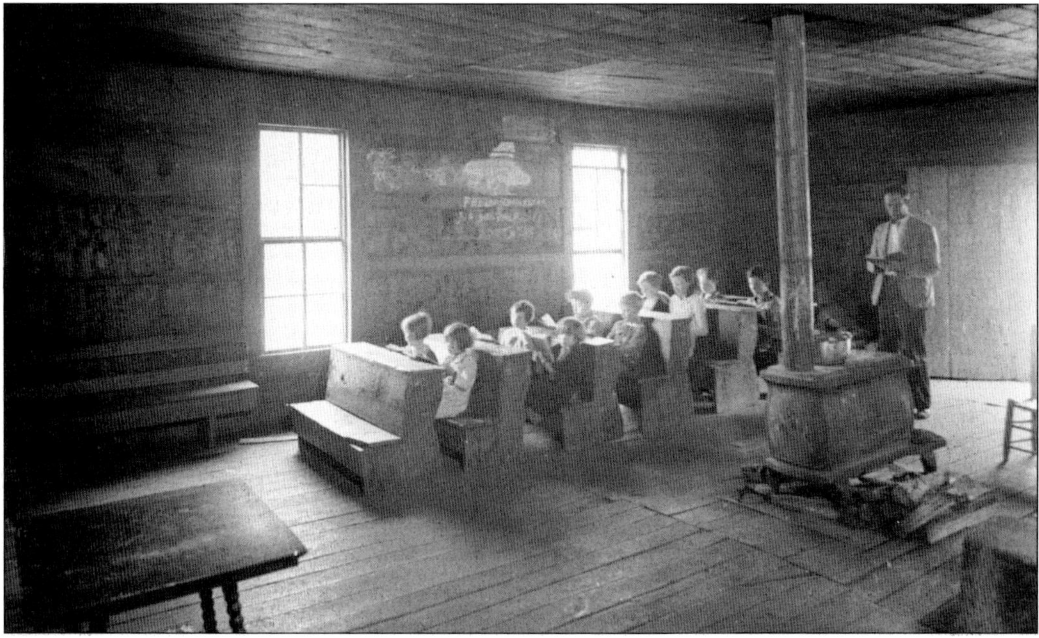

This is the 1935–1936 school picture taken by E.E. Exline. Pictured are (first bench from left) Margaret Tallent and Mary Moore; (second bench) Rowena Tallent and Betty Moore; (third bench) Conley Russell and unidentified; (fourth bench) two unidentified; (fifth bench) unidentified and John Moore. Teacher Herman Matthews is standing at far right. (Courtesy Great Smoky Mountains National Park archives.)

Three

Little Greenbrier Church

At one time, most public buildings served multiple purposes, and the Little Greenbrier School was no exception, functioning as a church and social hall as well as a school. Church services were held on Sundays for the Primitive Baptist faith. Prayer meetings were also held on weekday nights.

Primitive Baptists generally do not use musical instruments during services, believing that all church music should instead be sung, because there is no New Testament command to play instruments, only to sing. The King James version of the Bible is the only version recognized by the Primitive Baptist church.

No musical instruments were used in the services at the Little Greenbrier Church. Shape note music was the method of worship in song and remains popular today in the area. Shape note singing is frequently held in area churches for those who still enjoy this practice.

For Primitive Baptists, baptism is the means of induction into the church. Elders conduct baptisms and rebaptize a person who was baptized by another denomination. Full immersion in water is the method used.

When the congregation outgrew the original Little Greenbrier School in the 1920s, a much bigger clapboard church was built close by. The bell from the original building was moved to the new church.

The majority of inhabitants of the Little Greenbrier community were of the Primitive Baptist faith. Those belonging to any other denomination would have had to travel a great distance to attend the service of their choice.

The original benches in the building were half a slab of log with four legs. One original bench remains in the school at this time. The second set of benches were made with straight backs, seats, and supporting lumber on the bottom. The third set are what visitors see at the school today—a back, seat, cubby in the back for books and slate boards, and a lumber bottom for its frame.

When the national park was established in 1934, the new church was dismantled, and the lumber was sold to the Friendship Baptist Church on Happy Hollow Road in Wears Valley.

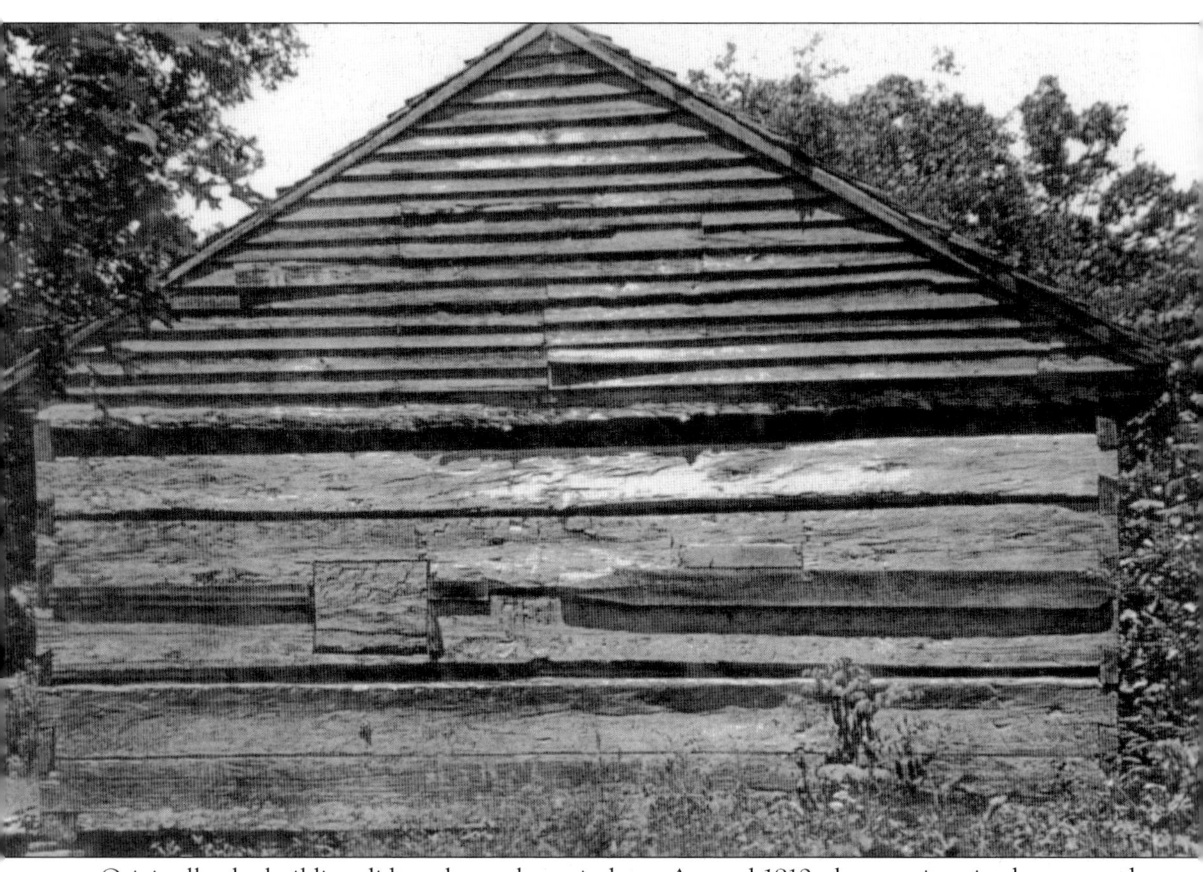

Originally, the building did not have glass windows. Around 1910, the openings in the east and west walls were enlarged, and the windows seen today were installed. The original blackboard was replaced at the same time. The square seen here on the rear, or south wall, was placed in what had been called the preacher's window since it provided light for the preacher (or the teacher, when class was in session). Unfortunately, the new blackboard covered this opening, so the preacher's window was filled in with a log that was removed when the other windows were enlarged. (Courtesy Great Smoky Mountains National Park archives.)

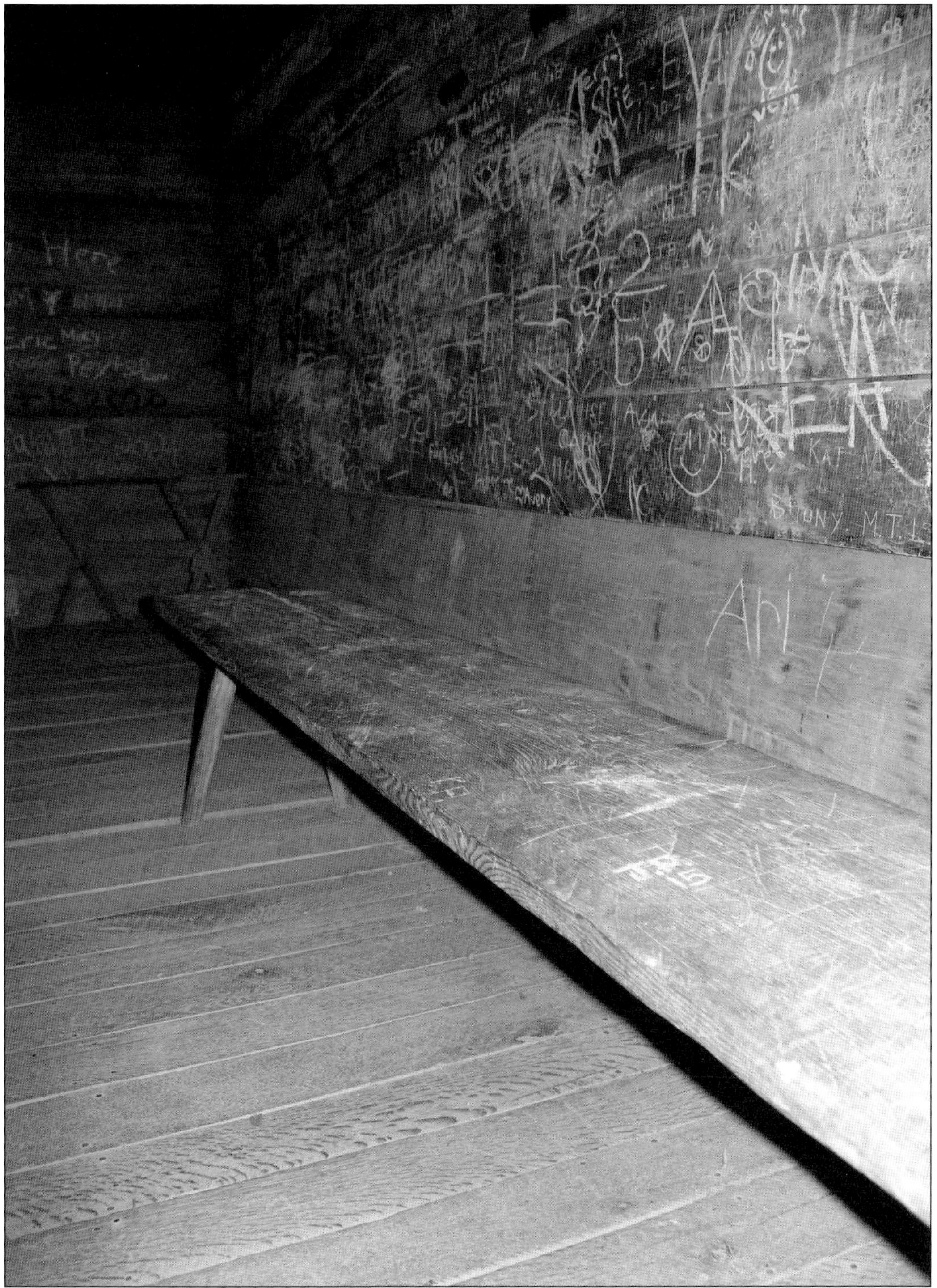

This is the original bench from 1882 that remains in the Little Greenbrier School as of 2021. The bench stayed pristine until the 2010s, when vandals and graffiti artists started defacing it. (Photograph by the author.)

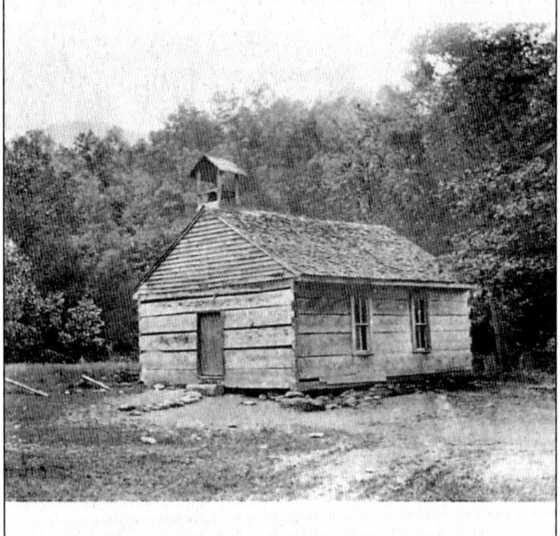

The cover of "Rememberin' The Little Greenbriar School and Primitive Baptist Church" by Margaret Stinnett Crabtree shows the belfry and bell when the booklet was published in the 1950s. Note the bottom board, which was replaced in the 2010s. (Courtesy Robin Goddard.)

This is an undated photograph of the congregation of the Little Greenbrier Church. It appears that the bell is still in the belfry, indicating that the picture was taken sometime before 1924. (Courtesy Great Smoky Mountains National Park archives.)

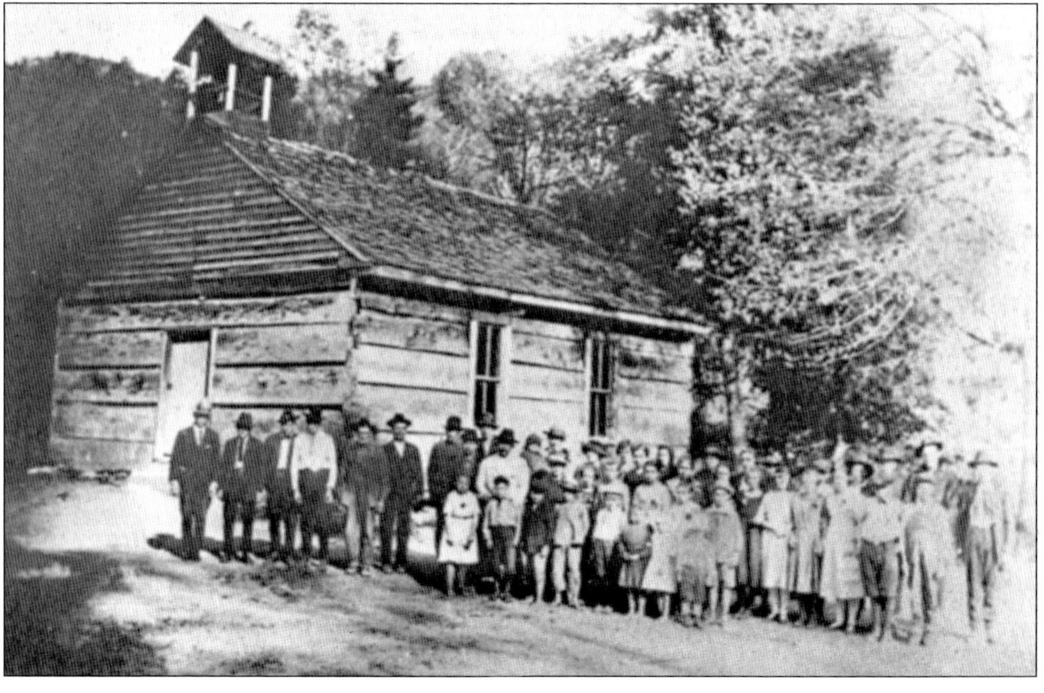

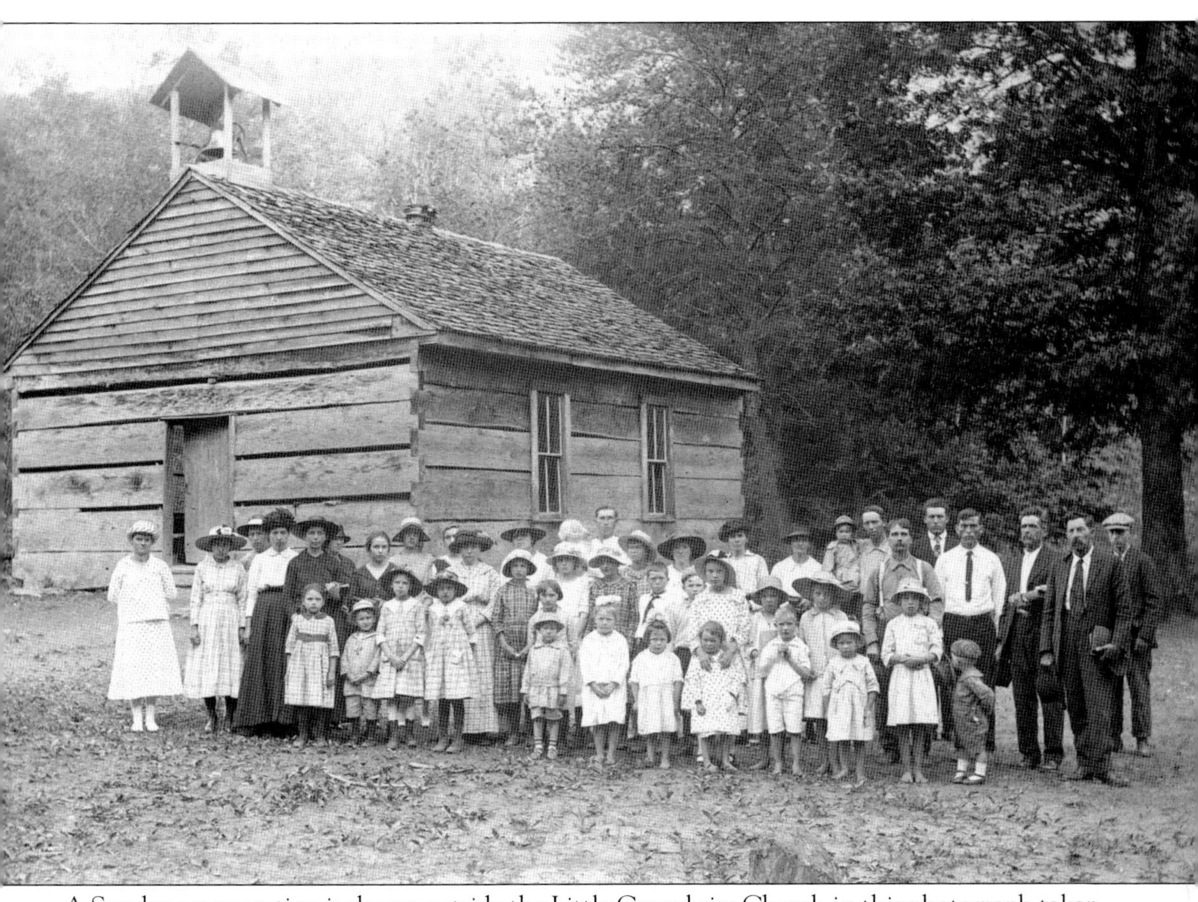

A Sunday congregation is shown outside the Little Greenbrier Church in this photograph taken sometime around 1917 or 1918. It is not often that images like this included a full list of names. Pictured here are from left to right, (first row) Hazel Shelton Hembree, John Shelton, Leona Shelton Cotter, Effie Shelton Phipps, Paul Abbott, Freddy Abbott, Josie Walker Ward, Marjorie Walker Shelton, Ruby Davis, Fred Walker, Genieva Stinnett, Pearl Walker Kirby, and Jack Griffitts; (second row) Caroline Walker Shelton, Lena Walker Hicks, Louisa Walker, Minnie Walker Maples, Evelyn Walker Abbott, Ethel Walker Maples, Frank Walker, Lyman Abbott, Edith Davis Sutton, Iva Davis Leonard, and Lucy Walker Tallent; (third row) Nora Reese Metcalf, Nora Walker, Hettie Walker, Martha Walker, Zala Abbott Griffitts, Willie Abbott, Alice Walker, Mary Jane Walker Abbott, John Andrew Abbott, Gene Abbott, Addie Reese Davis, Ethel Andrew Wilkerson, Martha Jane Walker, Maude Abbott, Jim Abbott, John H. Walker, Tom Abbott, John Stinnett Jr., Wiley Walker, Elder John J. Abbott, George Walker, Wiley Walker, and Elder John H. Abbott, pastor of Headrick Chapel Church. (Courtesy Great Smoky Mountains National Park archives.)

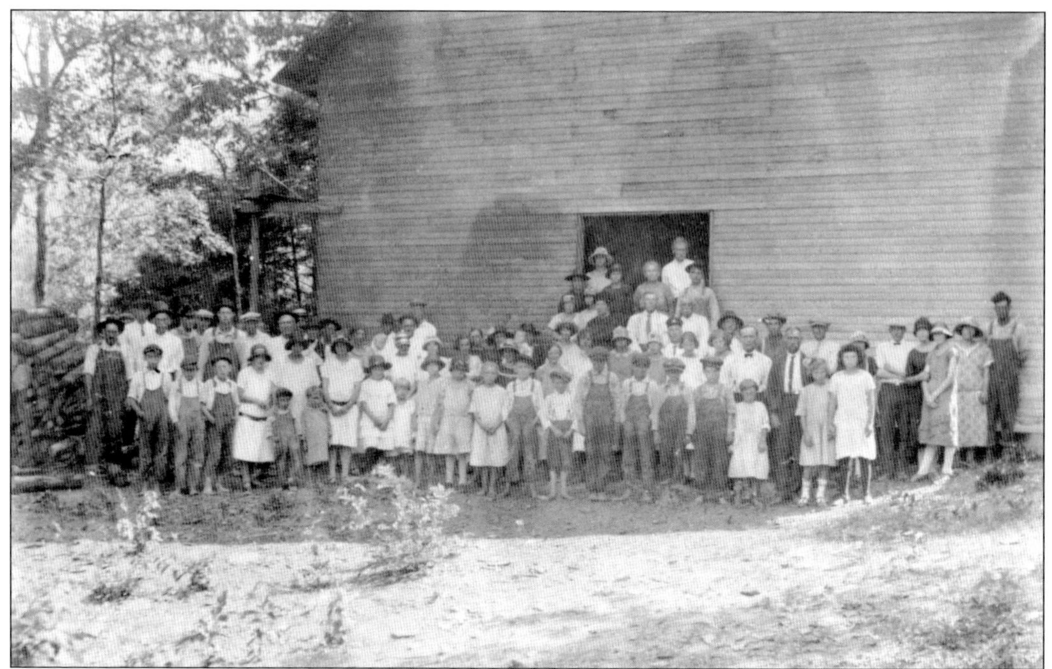

The new Little Greenbrier Church, built in 1924, is pictured in this photograph taken by Jim Shelton sometime between 1925 and 1927. The land for the new church was donated by Tine Metcalf. After Great Smoky Mountains National Park was established, this church was dismantled and moved to Wears Valley to help build the Friendship Baptist Church on Happy Hollow Road (Courtesy Great Smoky Mountains National Park archives.)

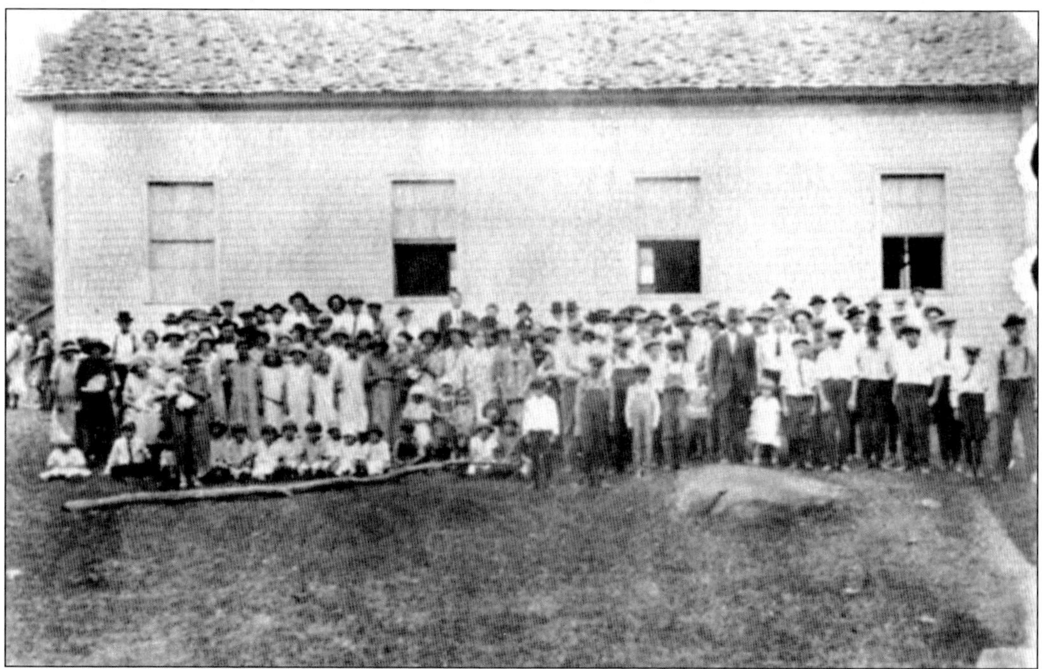

This image is from "Rememberin' the Little Greenbriar School and Primitive Baptist Church" by Margaret Stinnett Crabtree. No date was noted. (Courtesy Robin Goddard.)

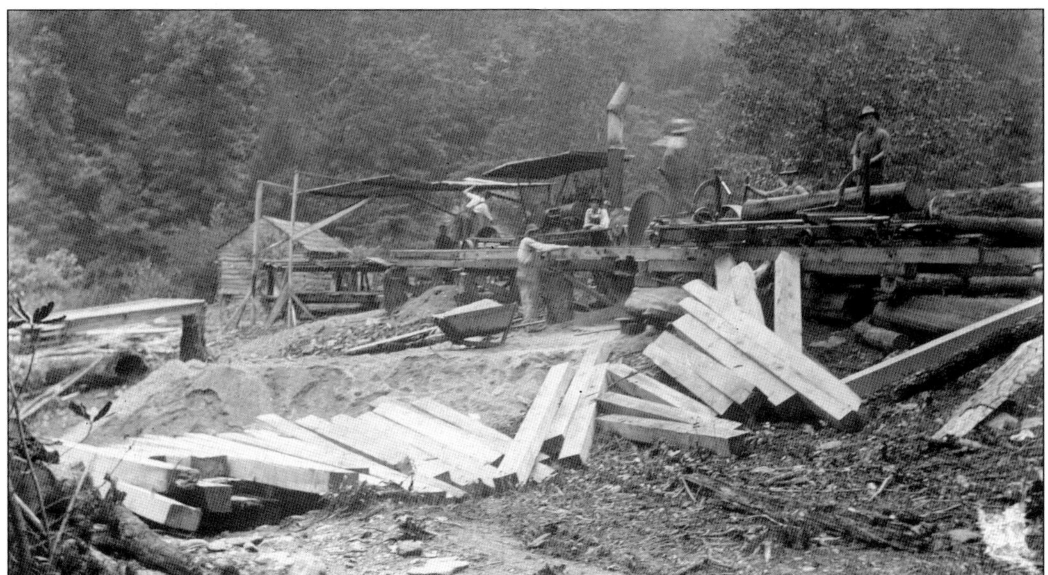

The wood for the new clapboard church came from the mill in Little Greenbrier. This photograph by Jim Shelton dates to 1900. (Courtesy Great Smoky Mountains National Park archives.)

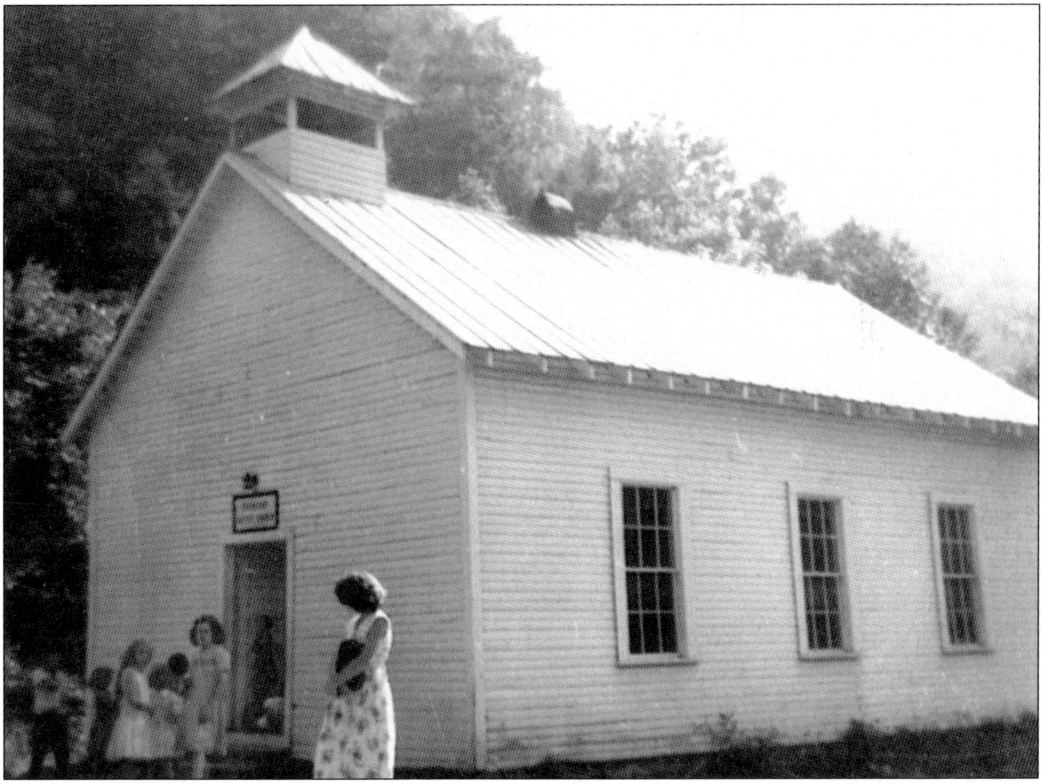

Wood from the second Little Greenbrier Church was used to construct the Friendship Baptist Church (pictured) on Happy Hollow Road in Wears Valley. The wooden Friendship Baptist Church was torn down around 1974 and replaced with a new concrete church across the road. The new church, in turn, replaced the Park Settlement School in that location. (Courtesy Jean Teaster.)

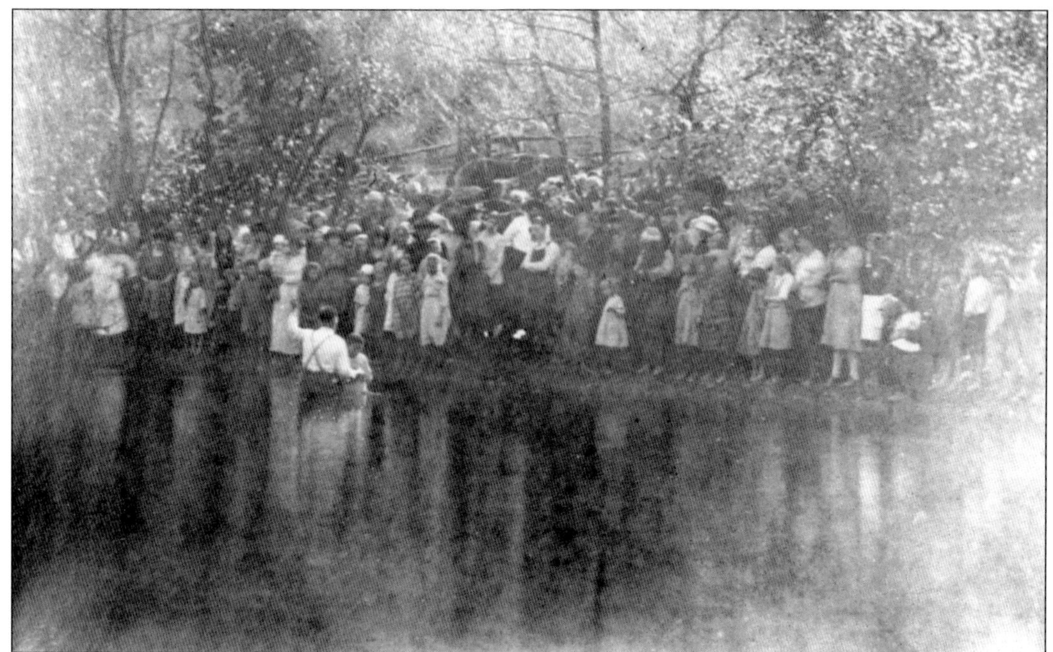

Hazel Shelton, daughter of Sarah Caroline and James Shelton, is shown being baptized in the Little River. The baptizing hole is still visible where there are 10 parking places across the Little River Road from Metcalf Bottoms toward Sugarlands Visitor Center. (Courtesy Great Smoky Mountains National Park archives.)

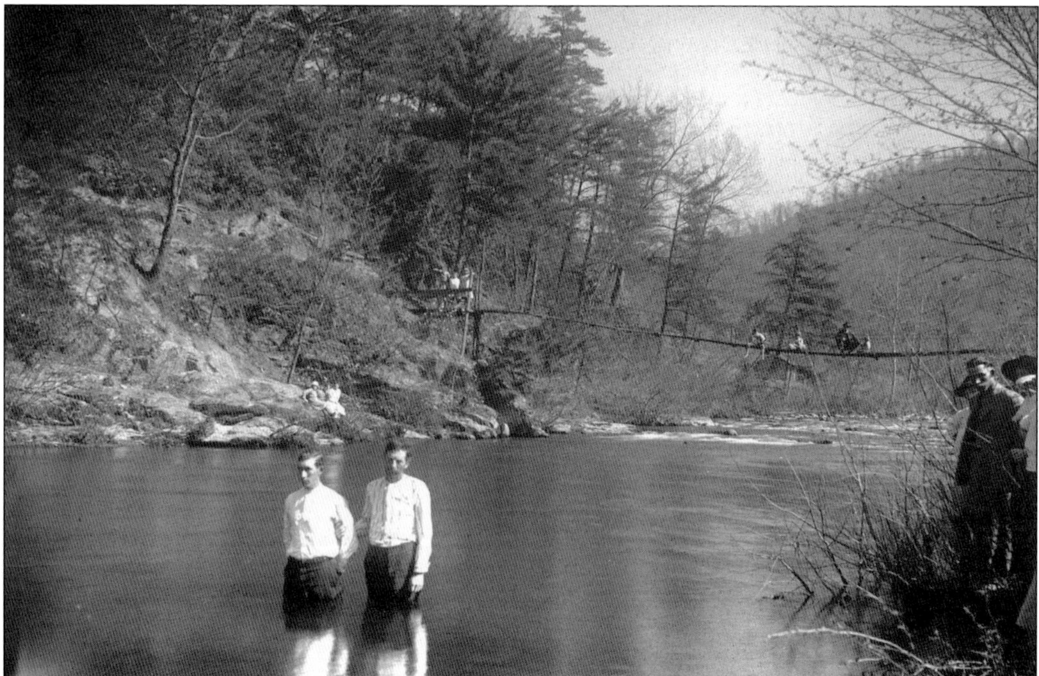

John Abbot Jr. is shown being baptized by his uncle Elder Dan Abbott in the Little River near Little Greenbrier. Note the swinging bridge in the background. (Courtesy Great Smoky Mountains National Park archives.)

Four

The Master Plan

When the national park was established in 1934, it was decided that all residents of the Little Greenbrier area would be removed by 1936. Destruction of the buildings in the park commenced soon after. A few homesteads were allowed lifetime leases in which the person or family would be allowed to stay in their home until the time of their death, when the land/house would revert to the national park; the Walker sisters, who lived 1.1 miles up the road from the Little Greenbrier School, were members of one of these families.

The last unmarried Walker sister, Louisa, passed away in 1964. The family was quite adamant that neither their house nor the school should be torn down, and they frequently spoke to park officials to try to make sure the buildings would be preserved.

When interviewed by Adele McKinzie, Jim Shelton stated that the "schoolhouse stood empty and unchanged until the aftermath of World War II. During this time, the structure began to deteriorate, and the forest began to close in on it."

By 1948, Great Smoky Mountains National Park was able to perform some maintenance and repairs on the school. In the spring of 1952, a group of families showed up for an old fashioned "workin'," and thanks to them, the grounds were clean for a homecoming at the Little Greenbrier School.

The National Park Service vacillated while figuring out what to do with the building. In 1955, NPS director Conrad Wirth proposed a plan named Mission 66. This was a 10-year program that would start in 1956 and end in 1966. Pres. Dwight Eisenhower accepted the plan and authorized the secretary of the interior to present it to Congress for approval. The goal of Mission 66 was to upgrade facilities and build additional and better structures in national parks and fund areas that needed attention. In Great Smoky Mountains National Park, two main structures were built—the Clingsmans Dome observation tower and the Sugarlands Visitor Center.

By 1962, Mission 66 was in full swing. Much preservation work was done, along with rehabilitation and new construction. If not for this initiative, the attention by the former Little Greenbrier community, and the efforts of Margaret Elsie Burrell ("Miss Elsie") in the late 1960s, the schoolhouse might not exist today. Miss Elsie presented a proposal to the national park that would allow her to present a program about the building to visitors. The proposal was accepted, and programs began in June 1970 and continue to this day.

UNITED STATES
DEPARTMENT OF THE INTERIOR
NATIONAL PARK SERVICE
EASTERN DIVISION, BRANCH OF PLANS AND DESIGN

Great Smoky Mountains National Park,
Gatlinburg, Tennessee,
July 17, 1935

Memo to Mr. Ludgate:

About one month ago I visited the log school house in Little Greenbrier Cove. This is one of the most interesting and unique buildings in the Park. It is an exceptionally fine building, 24' x 30', built of poplar logs, five logs high, the logs averaging about 24" in width. The building was used as a school during the past winter. The original benches which were in use at that time have been moved to the church nearby. This building is the only log school house I have seen or heard of in the Park.

Yesterday I visited this building with Mr. Exline to take photographs of it. I found the building had been vandalized to a considerable extent. Most of the glass in the windows and some of the sash had been broken, and the stove torn down and broken. Stove wood stacked in the rear of the room had caught on fire and several of these pieces had been hurled through the windows.

In speaking to Mr. Dunn, Assistant Chief Ranger, I learned that the people living in this section are rough and have no respect for property. This building is frequented by natives for gambling and drinking, these activities frequently resulting in fights and brawls. The building is located about three-quarters of a mile off Hwy. 73, making it impossible to give it adequate protection.

In view of the uniqueness of this building, the danger of its destruction by vandalism and fire, I recommend that this building be razed as soon as possible after an adequate number of photographs and drawings can be made; that all members of the building be carefully numbered, said numbers to agree with numbers placed on corresponding members as indicated on the drawings; that the materials of the building be stored in some safe place protected from the weather until such time as a suitable place can be selected for its reconstruction.

Charles S. Grossman,
Architectural Foreman.

p
cc Mr. Eakin
Mr. Peterson

The letter at left from Charles Grossman to a Mr. Ludgate is dated July 17, 1935, and states Grossman's wishes to tear down the schoolhouse. One might question his assumptions of the community, as the locals were strictly Primitive Baptist. It is doubtful that the local population would destroy their beloved school and church. Just a few days later, on July 21, 1935, the below memorandum from Alden Stevens said that the building should be preserved. (Both, courtesy Great Smoky Mountains National Park archives.)

LITTLE GREENBRIER SCHOOLHOUSE - Building No. 129

Alden B. Stevens, Museum Curator.

Sunday, July 21, 1935

Went with Mr. Charles Grossman, architectural foreman, to visit the old schoolhouse at Little Greenbrier. This was built 53 years ago as a community project without state or county aid; and has been used for classes up until last winter. It is one of the finest log buildings in the park area, and is in fair condition, though it has been damaged by vandals. The old hand made desks and benches are still in the building. Mr. Grossman and I both felt that this was one of the buildings which should certainly be preserved.

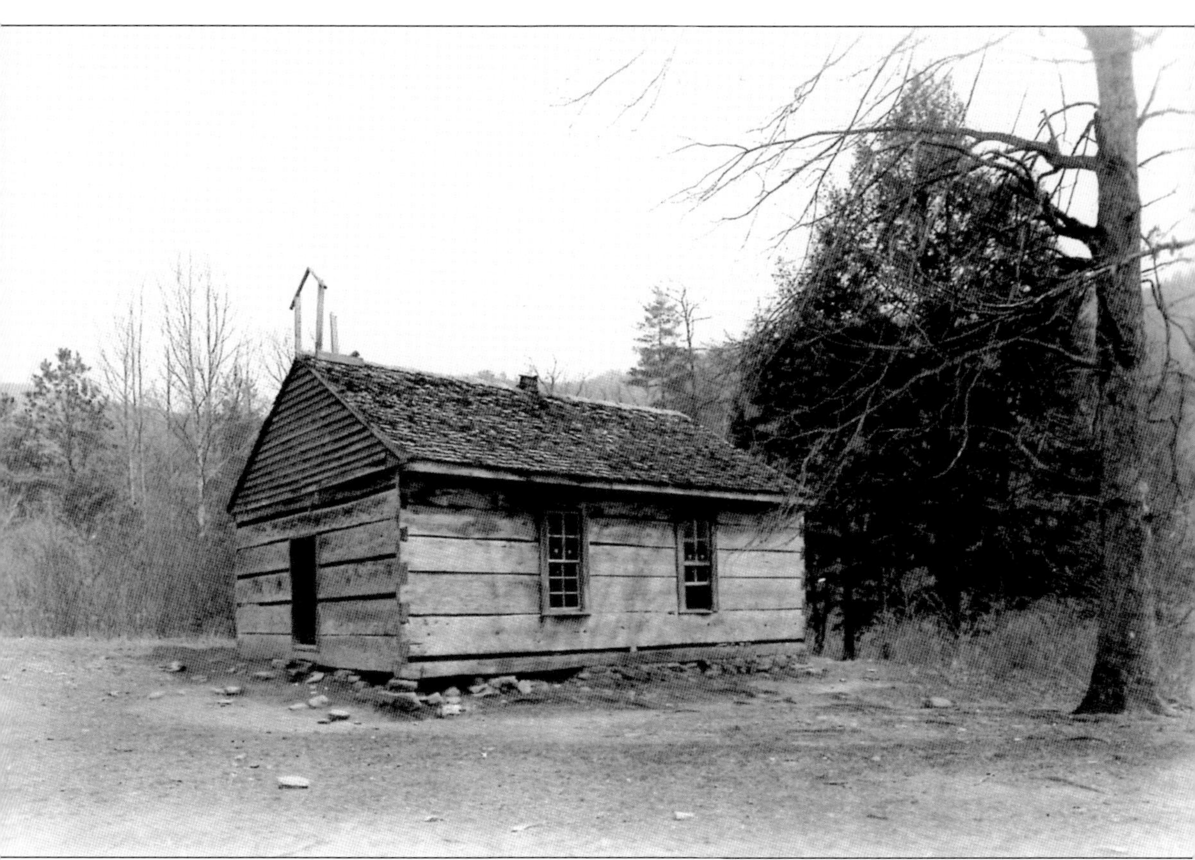

This view of the Little Greenbrier School shows part of the belfry without the bell. The date must be after 1924, when the bell was placed in the new church in Little Greenbrier. (Courtesy Great Smoky Mountains National Park archives.)

PIONEER STRUCTURES GREAT SMOKY MOUNTAINS NATIONAL PARK

ne of Group: Little Green Brier Name of Building: School house Location: Little Green Brie

of Information:

Material: ________ shakes, boards; Length: ________ Maximum & Minimum width: ________

posure to the weather: ________ Number of courses on each side: ________

placements made: Date: July 1, 1948

Two new locust sills put under house, first old in rear of house spliced with new piece 16 square heavy screen wire vent in each window shutter, roof repaired, gables repaired, over head raised and braced.

ems removed and stored: Tag No. ________ Storage House Location: ________

None

ems treated with preservative:

etches made by: ________ Date: Aug. 6, 1948

ot plans prepared on H.A.B.S. Sheets by: ________ Date: ________

Information on this card by: M. O. Henderson Date: ________

Detailed notes were made every time repairs were done. Surprisingly, considering the post-war economy and the fact that the future of the school was uncertain at the time, these repairs were done in 1948. (Courtesy Great Smoky Mountains National Park archives.)

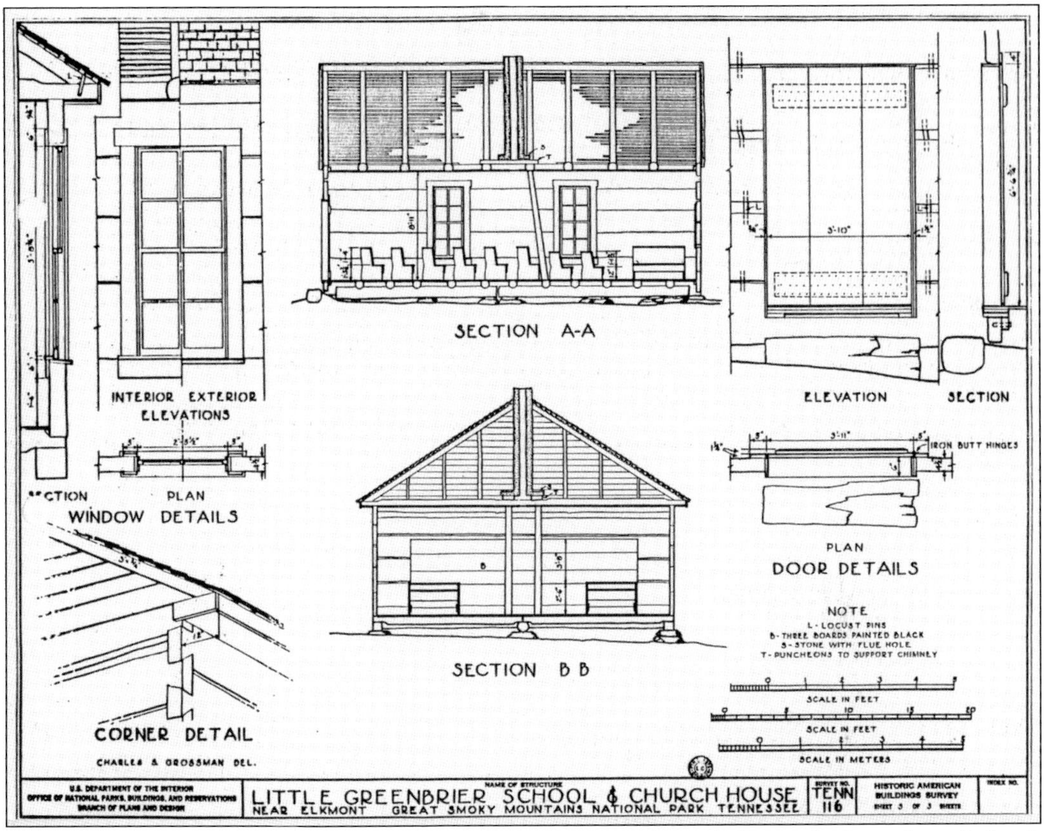

When the National Park Service began to consider what to do with the Little Greenbrier School, destruction of the building was a possibility. Later, NPS representatives considered disassembling the building and erecting it elsewhere in the park. Detailed drawings and measurements were taken for use in a future reconstruction of the building. The preacher's window was not shown on the drawings. (Courtesy Great Smoky Mountains National Park archives.)

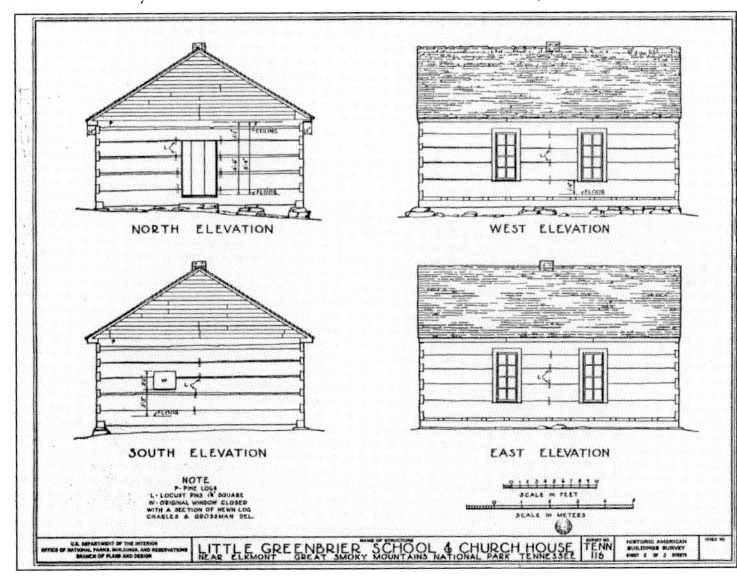

Detailed drawings were made of the four elevations of the school for future use. (Courtesy Great Smoky Mountains National Park archives.)

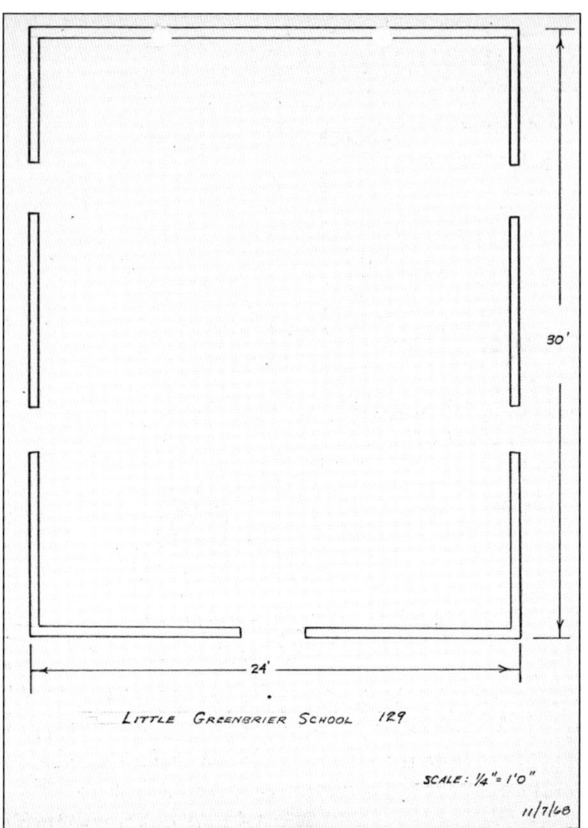

Four walls, four windows, and one door comprised the complete school. This drawing of the Little Greenbrier School is about as simple as a plan can be. (Courtesy Great Smoky Mountains National Park archives.)

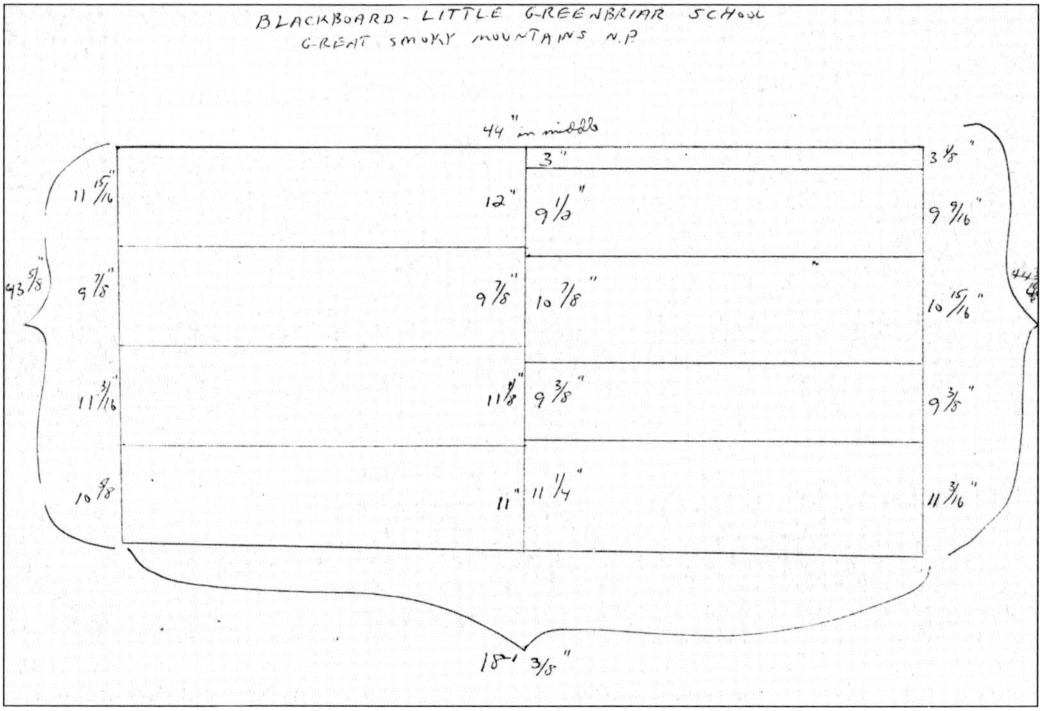

Even the blackboard was measured and diagrammed to prepare for the potential destruction of the building. The blackboard was a literal interpretation of the word—boards painted black. The children used slate boards for their personal schoolwork. (Courtesy Great Smoky Mountains National Park archives.)

BLACKBOARD - LITTLE GREENBRIAR SCHOOL
GREAT SMOKY MOUNTAINS N.P

44" in middle

18' 3/8"

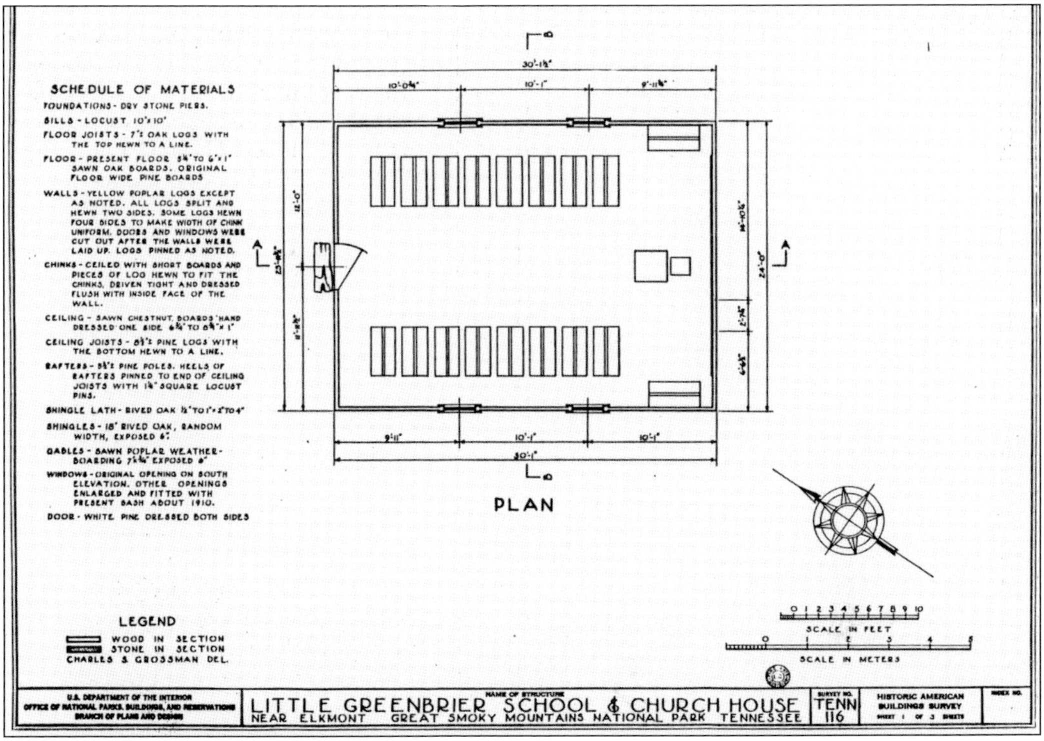

SCHEDULE OF MATERIALS

FOUNDATIONS - DRY STONE PIERS.

SILLS - LOCUST 10"x10"

FLOOR JOISTS - 7"± OAK LOGS WITH THE TOP HEWN TO A LINE.

FLOOR - PRESENT FLOOR 5¼" TO 6"x1" SAWN OAK BOARDS. ORIGINAL FLOOR WIDE PINE BOARDS

WALLS - YELLOW POPLAR LOGS EXCEPT AS NOTED. ALL LOGS SPLIT AND HEWN TWO SIDES. SOME LOGS HEWN FOUR SIDES TO MAKE WIDTH OF CHINK UNIFORM. DOORS AND WINDOWS WERE CUT OUT AFTER THE WALLS WERE LAID UP. LOGS PINNED AS NOTED.

CHINKS - CEILED WITH SHORT BOARDS AND PIECES OF LOG HEWN TO FIT THE CHINKS, DRIVEN TIGHT AND DRESSED FLUSH WITH INSIDE FACE OF THE WALL.

CEILING - SAWN CHESTNUT BOARDS HAND DRESSED ONE SIDE 6¾" TO 8¾"x1"

CEILING JOISTS - 8½"± PINE LOGS WITH THE BOTTOM HEWN TO A LINE.

RAFTERS - 5½"± PINE POLES. HEELS OF RAFTERS PINNED TO END OF CEILING JOISTS WITH 1¼" SQUARE LOCUST PINS.

SHINGLE LATH - RIVED OAK ½" TO 1"x2" TO 4"

SHINGLES - 18" RIVED OAK, RANDOM WIDTH, EXPOSED 6".

GABLES - SAWN POPLAR WEATHER-BOARDING 7¼" EXPOSED 6"

WINDOWS - ORIGINAL OPENING ON SOUTH ELEVATION. OTHER OPENINGS ENLARGED AND FITTED WITH PRESENT SASH ABOUT 1910.

DOOR - WHITE PINE DRESSED BOTH SIDES

PLAN

LEGEND

WOOD IN SECTION
STONE IN SECTION
CHARLES S. GROSSMAN DEL.

SCALE IN FEET
SCALE IN METERS

U.S. DEPARTMENT OF THE INTERIOR
OFFICE OF NATIONAL PARKS, BUILDINGS, AND RESERVATIONS
BRANCH OF PLANS AND DESIGN

NAME OF STRUCTURE
LITTLE GREENBRIER SCHOOL & CHURCH HOUSE
NEAR ELKMONT GREAT SMOKY MOUNTAINS NATIONAL PARK TENNESSEE

SURVEY NO. TENN 116

HISTORIC AMERICAN BUILDINGS SURVEY
SHEET 1 OF 3 SHEETS

INDEX NO.

This drawing even included the benches and the podium into the master plan and included a list of the materials used in the building. (Courtesy Great Smoky Mountains National Park archives.)

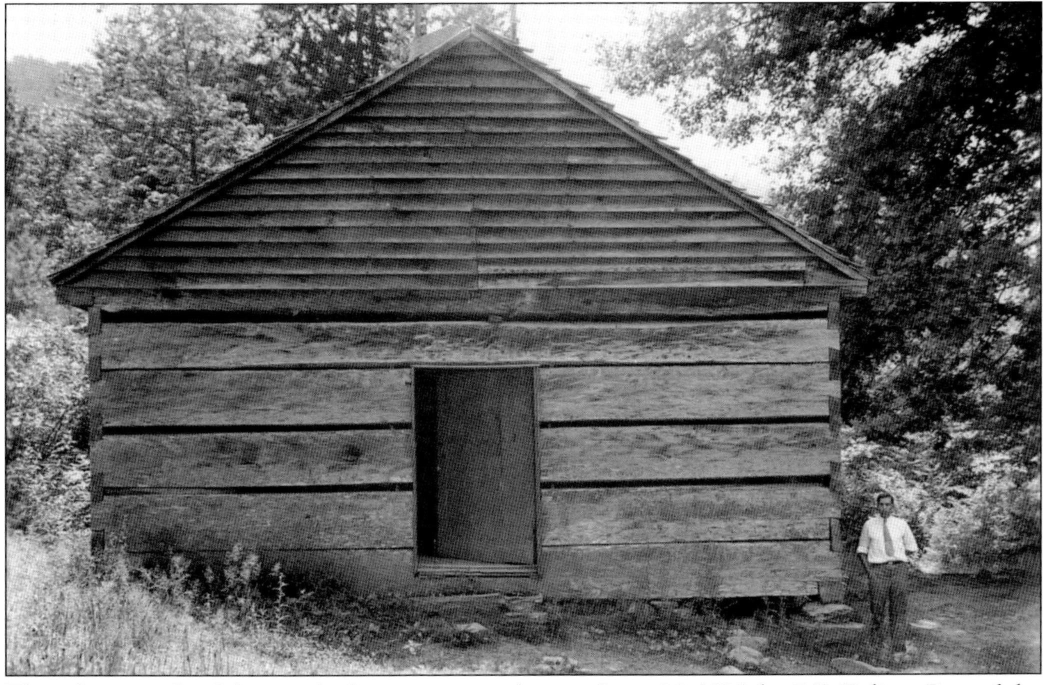

This photograph of the north elevation was taken on June 16, 1935, by E.E. Exline. Part of the belfry is still in place on the roof. (Courtesy Great Smoky Mountains National Park archives.)

Little Greenbrier School 129

PCP-297 (8/65) was to dismantle the building, move, and re-erect, replacing all unsound materials and treating all wood with preservative. Now the thinking is to rehabilitate the structure at its present site.

This 1965 note indicated the desire to rehabilitate the school at its present site. Presumably around this time, Margaret "Miss Elsie" Burrell was formulating her plan to present park programs at the school. (Courtesy Great Smoky Mountains National Park archives.)

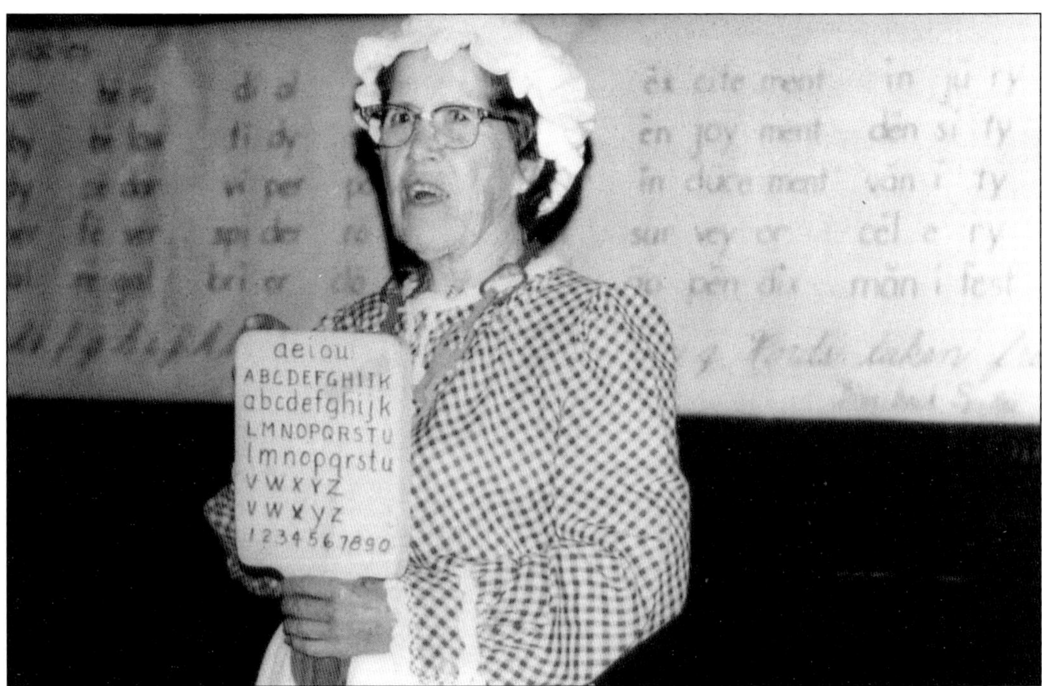

Miss Elsie created the curriculum for the park program at the Little Greenbrier School. It included subjects originally taught in the school, how the building was made and what tools were used, and information about local families. (Courtesy Great Smoky Mountains National Park archives.)

Five

Homecomings and Singing Schools

The Little Greenbrier homecomings started in 1951, and after that time, former residents got together to have a "workin'," or cleanup, of the school. In a note dated March 20, 1953, and sent from Edward Hummel, the park superintendent, to Clyde Abbott, the National Park Service agreed to clean out enough space in the former playground to make 30 parking places. Today, on a busy homecoming or program day, parking is problematic, and vehicles overflow the lot down the road. Little Greenbrier homecomings are held on the fourth Sunday in July of each year.

Currently, singings at Little Greenbrier are held on the third Sunday of July of each year. Shape note singing, also known as old harp singing, is the norm now, with no instruments to accompany the voices. Most singings still follow the early American format. Singers are arranged facing each other in a "hollow square" with four sections (treble, alto, tenor/"lead," and bass). Participants alternate standing in the middle of the square to lead a song of their choice. The singers first sing the "shapes" (do, re, me, etc.), then follow with the words.

The New Harp of Columbia states,

> In the small towns and rural areas of early America, church-sponsored "singing schools" proliferated as a way of both improving congregational singing and drawing communities together. Congregants attending these schools were taught a form of musical notation in which the notes were assigned different shapes to indicate variations in pitch—a method that worked well with singers having little understanding of standard musical notation. These schools eventually became major social events that drew hundreds of attendees, and today countless enthusiasts carry on the shape-note tradition.

According to oldharp.org, old harp singing is:

> not performance-based, nor is it typical of any choir or choral society. It is a participatory gathering where people sing for enjoyment. Although old harp singing dates back well over a century, the singings are not considered reenactments. They are events in which a living tradition continues to grow and thrive. Despite the passage of time, this style of music has endured because of its uniquely beautiful sound and the powerful bonds it creates between participants.

Margaret Stinnett Crabtree wrote a pamphlet entitled "Rememberin' The Little Greenbriar School and Primitive Baptist Church" for a 1950s reunion. Twenty some years after classes ceased being held at the school, she wrote, "Now this is a place of memories." Luckily for everyone, it was preserved and continues to make new memories for those who visit.

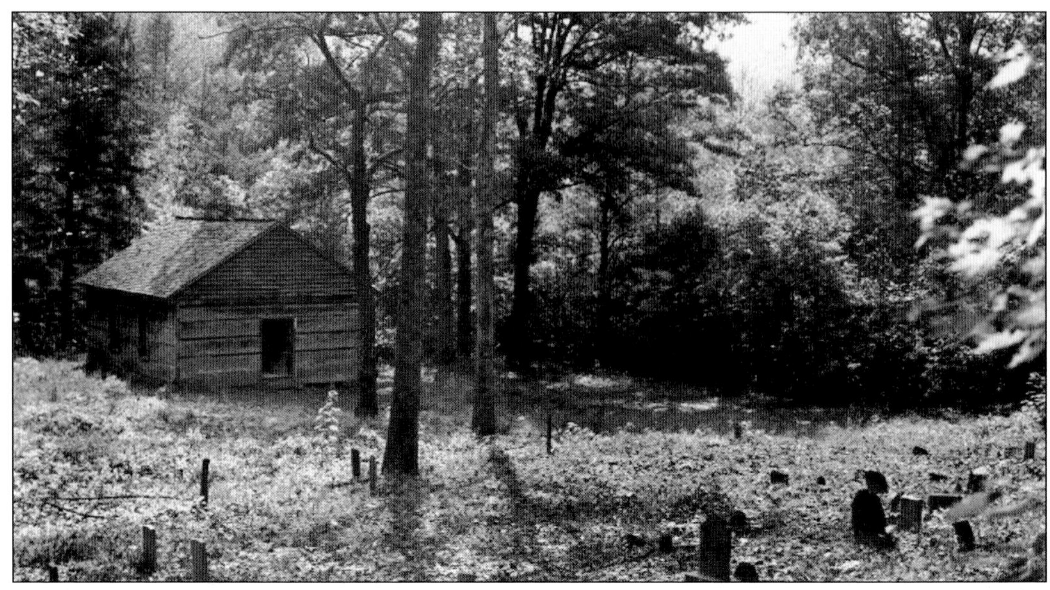

In these photographs by Albert Roth, the Little Greenbrier School's cemetery appears larger than it is now because of the lack of fencing. It appears that there were markers for graves closer to the school than today. (Both, courtesy University of Tennessee photograph archives.)

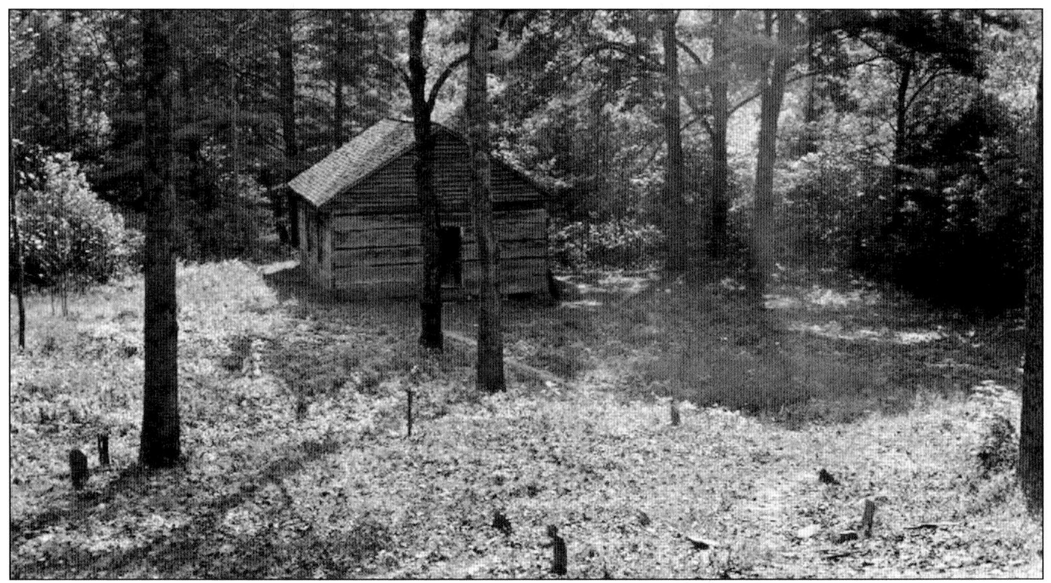

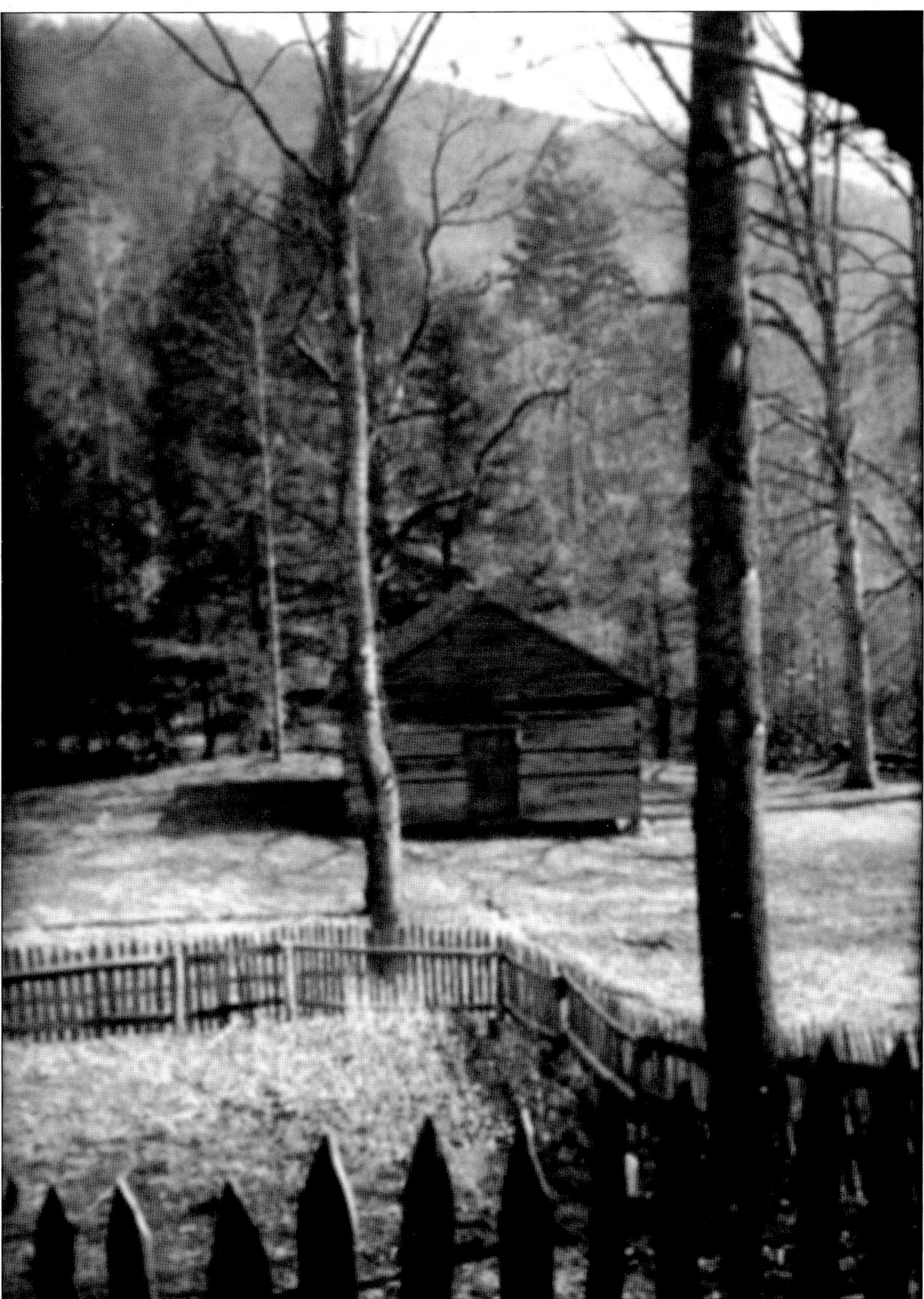

Trees were closer to the schoolhouse than they are now, and there were no worn paths crossing the stream or going to a nonexistent parking lot, as seen in this Albert Roth image. (Courtesy University of Tennessee photograph archives.)

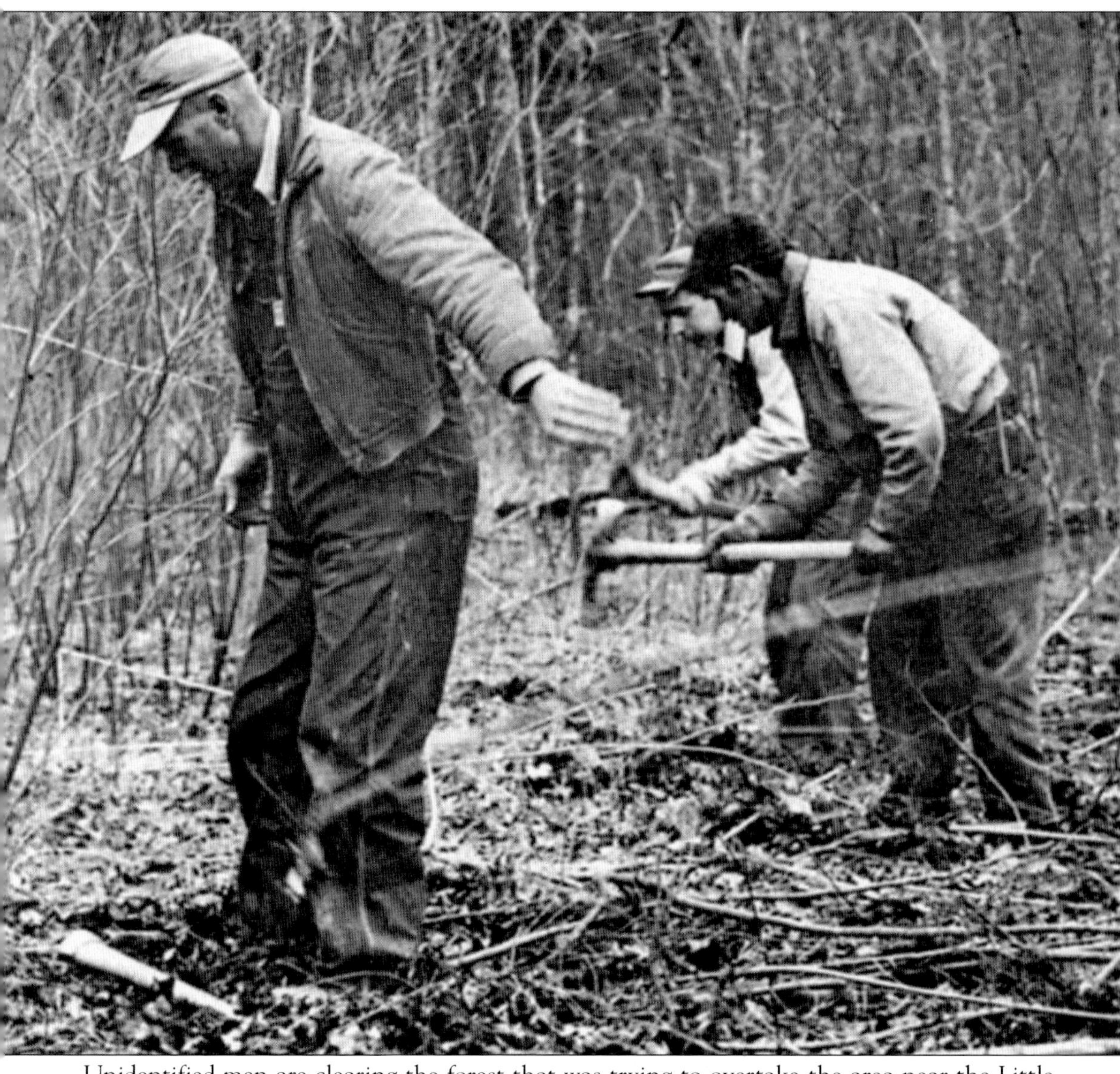

Unidentified men are clearing the forest that was trying to overtake the area near the Little Greenbrier School. The exact date of the photograph is unknown, but it must have been taken in the spring before the July homecoming. (Courtesy Great Smoky Mountains National Park archives.)

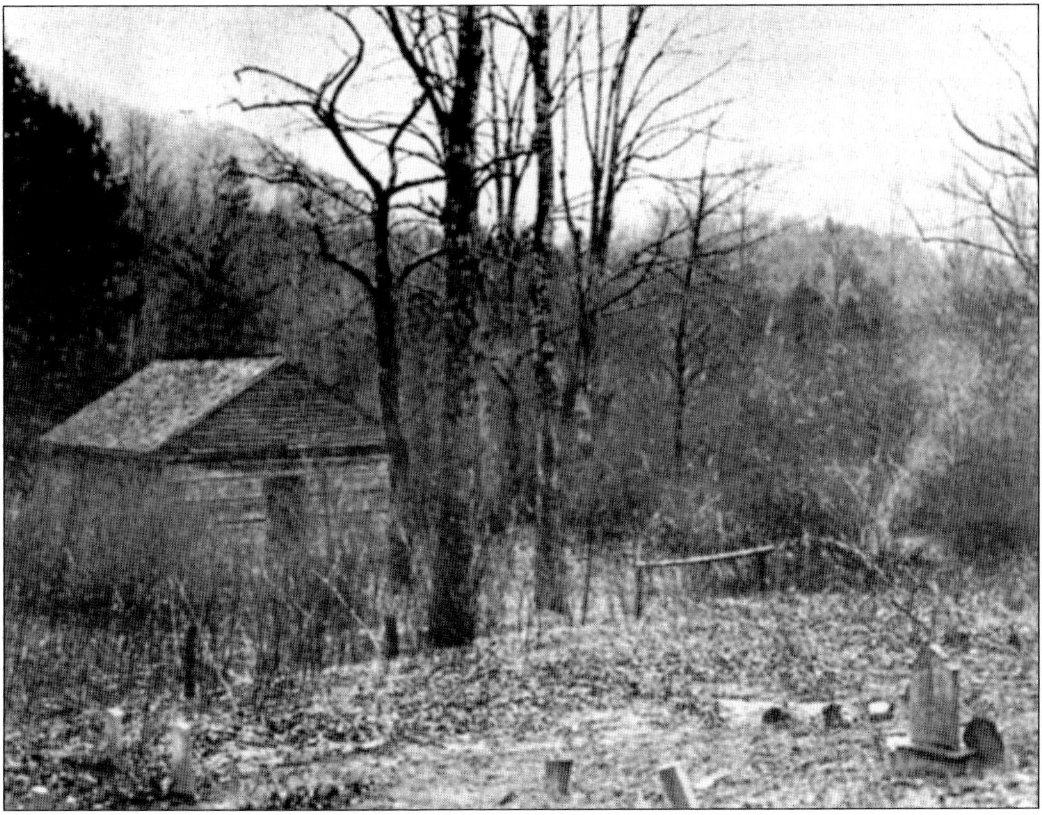

Cleanup began at the Little Greenbrier School in 1952. Note there is no fencing around the cemetery, or modern stones. (Courtesy Great Smoky Mountains National Park archives.)

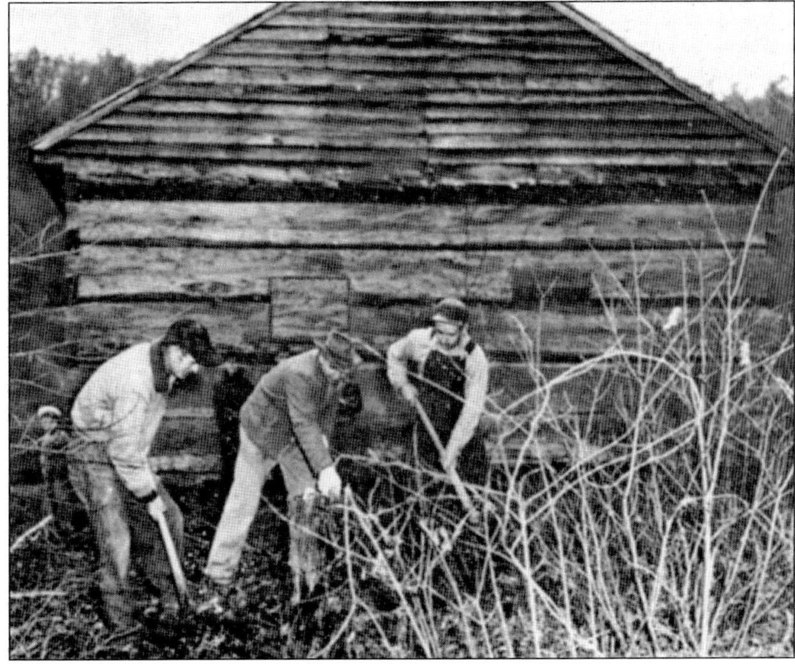

The south side of the school was quite overgrown until the "workin'." Tom Walker, Clyde Abbott, and Robert Walker are shown cleaning up the grounds. (Courtesy Great Smoky Mountains National Park archives.)

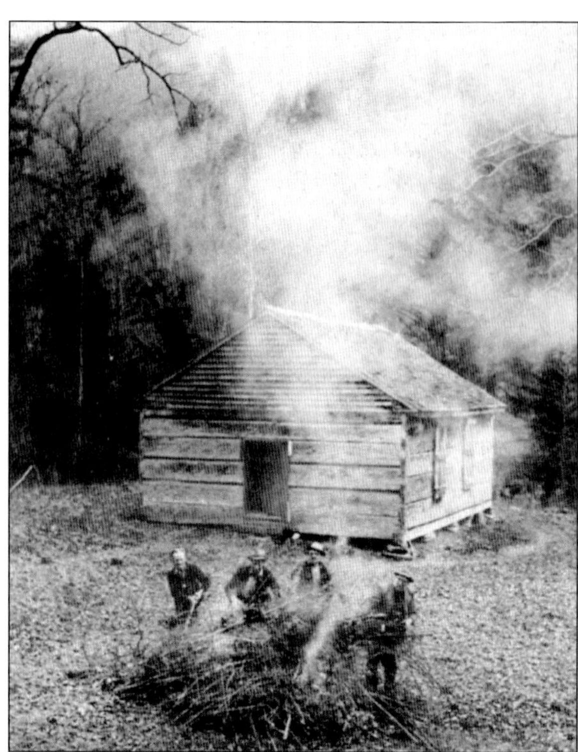

George Melton, Cary Oliver, Harrison Moore, and an unidentified person start the burn pile after the cleanup. Note that the belfry and chimney are both gone. (Courtesy Great Smoky Mountains National Park archives.)

A major cleanup job was undertaken at the Little Greenbrier School in 1952. The parking lot to the left had yet to be constructed when this photograph was taken. (Courtesy Great Smoky Mountains National Park archives.)

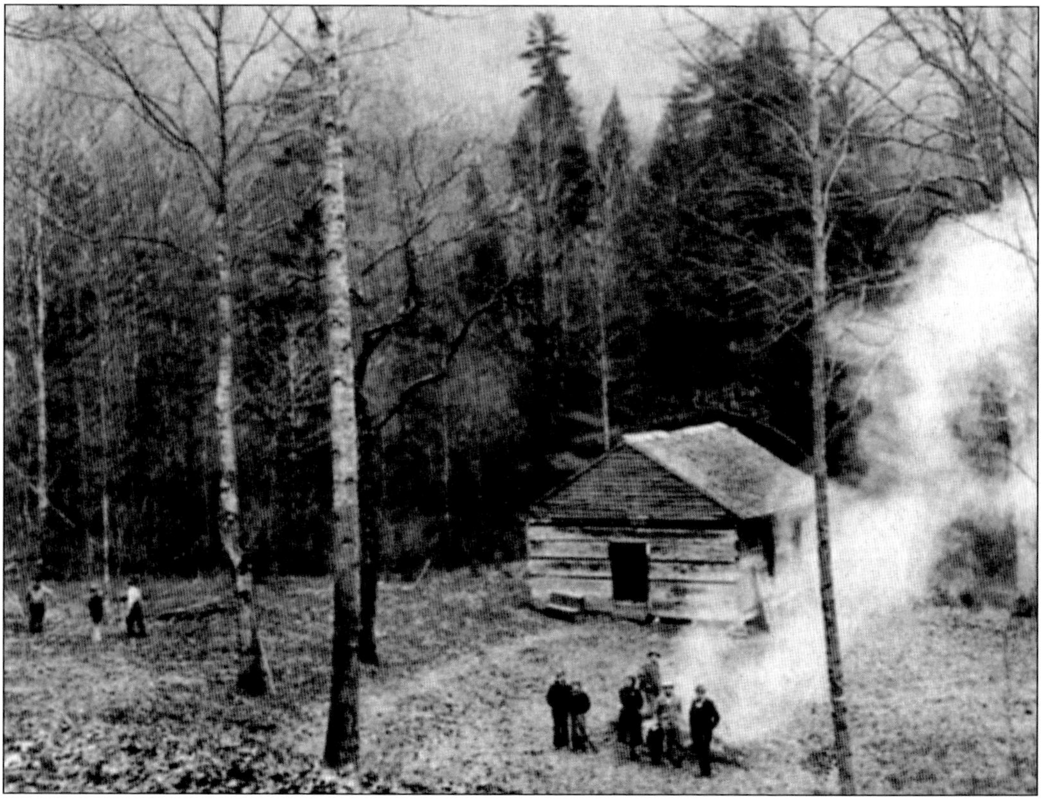

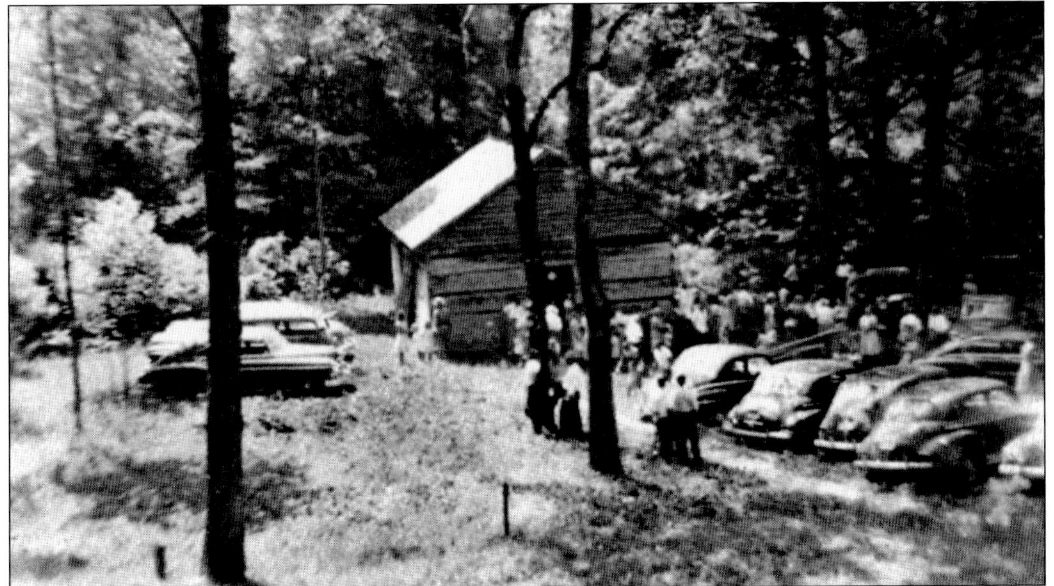

Since the parking lot was not yet created, cars were allowed to park very close to the school and cemetery. Note the poles in the foreground, possibly marking a grave. (Courtesy Great Smoky Mountains National Park archives.)

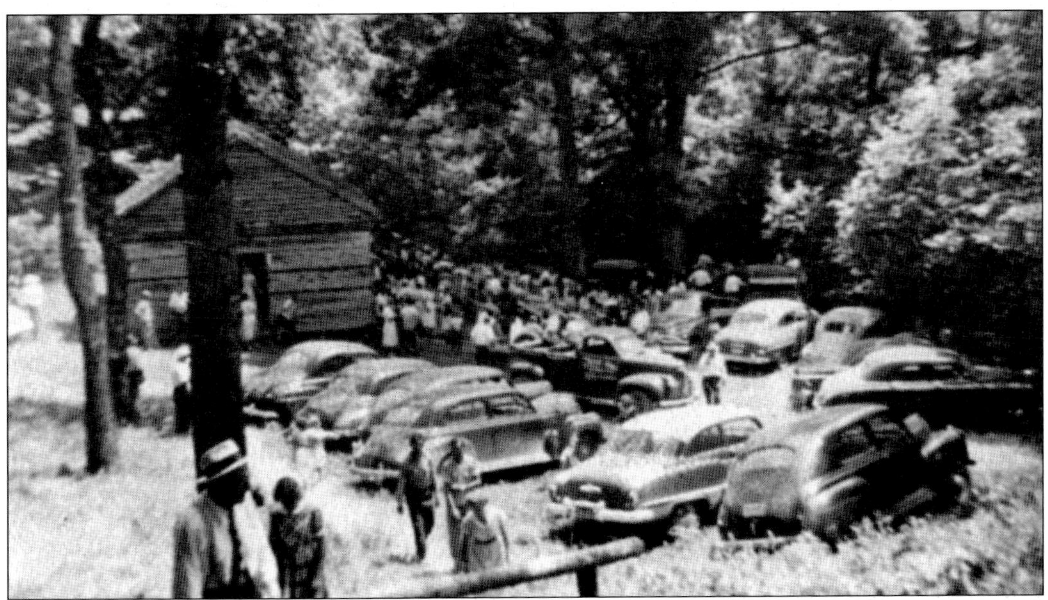

The 1952 homecoming saw many cars parked between the school and the cemetery. Note that there was no paling fence for the cemetery at this time. (Courtesy Great Smoky Mountains National Park archives.)

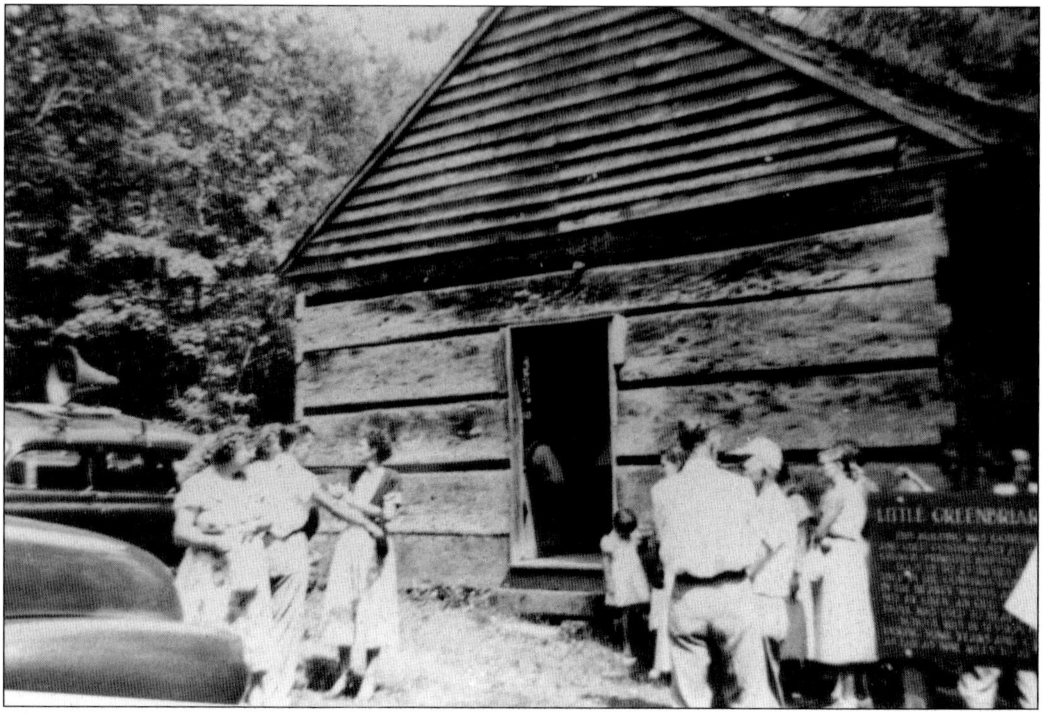

This is another photograph from the 1952 homecoming. It is not known when the sign was placed in front of the school, but it remained there well into the 1980s. (Courtesy Great Smoky Mountains National Park archives.)

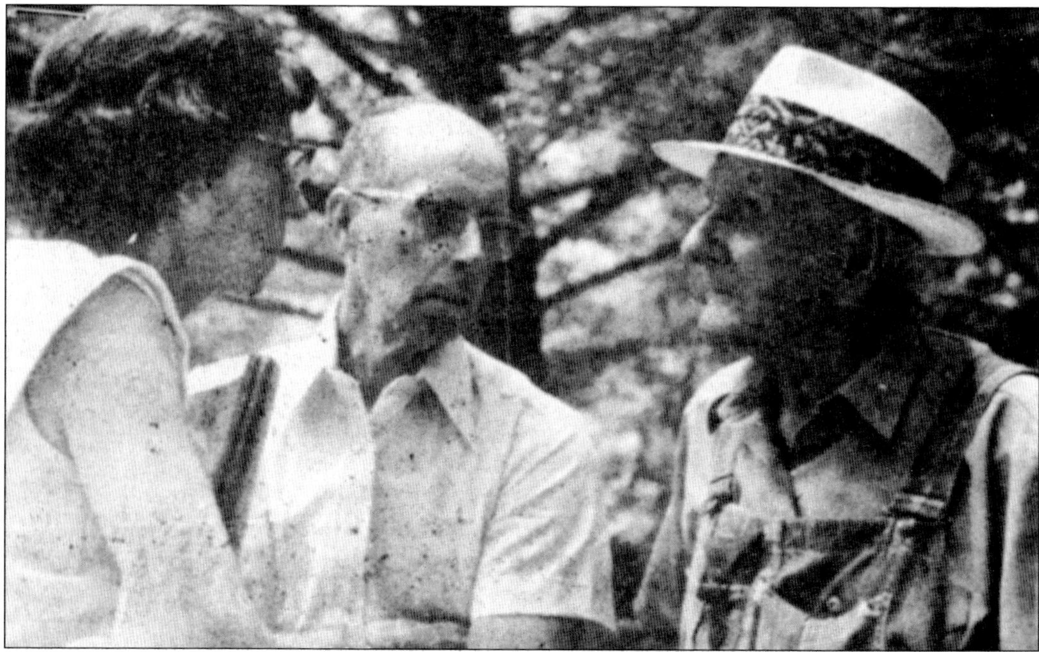

Roy Myers (right), former train conductor with the Little River Lumber Company, visits with friends at the July 17, 1977, homecoming event. (Courtesy Great Smoky Mountains National Park archives.)

Margaret Elsie Burrell looks at a historic book with two youngsters at a homecoming. (Courtesy Great Smoky Mountains National Park archives.)

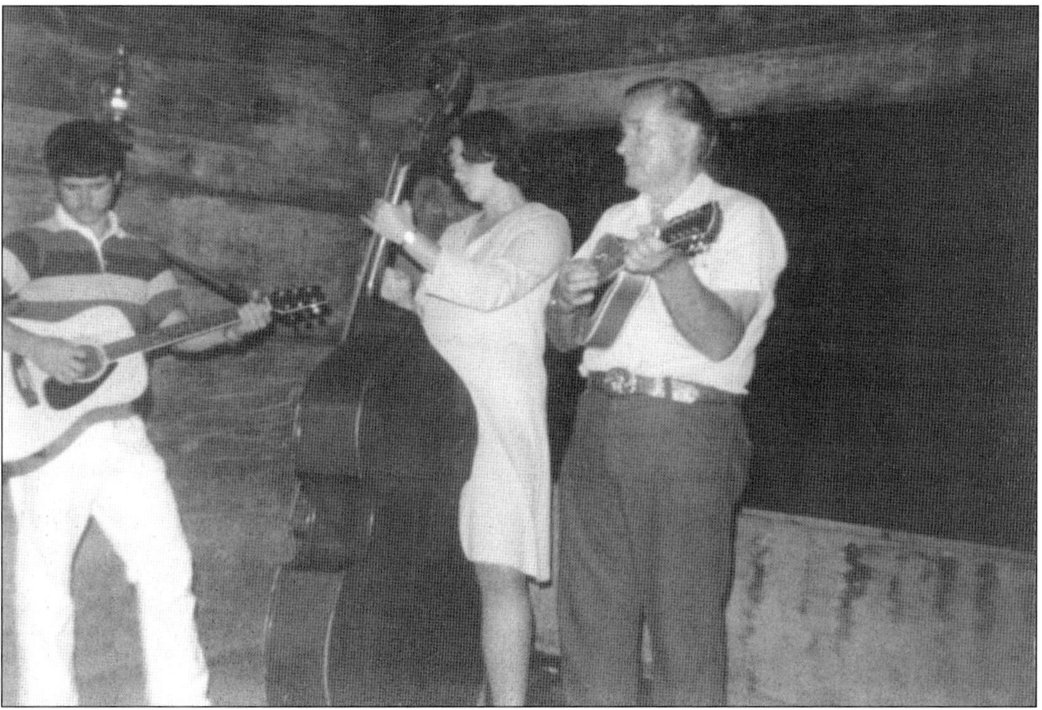

A band struck up some music at a homecoming. Music was incorporated into many homecomings over the years. (Courtesy Great Smoky Mountains National Park archives.)

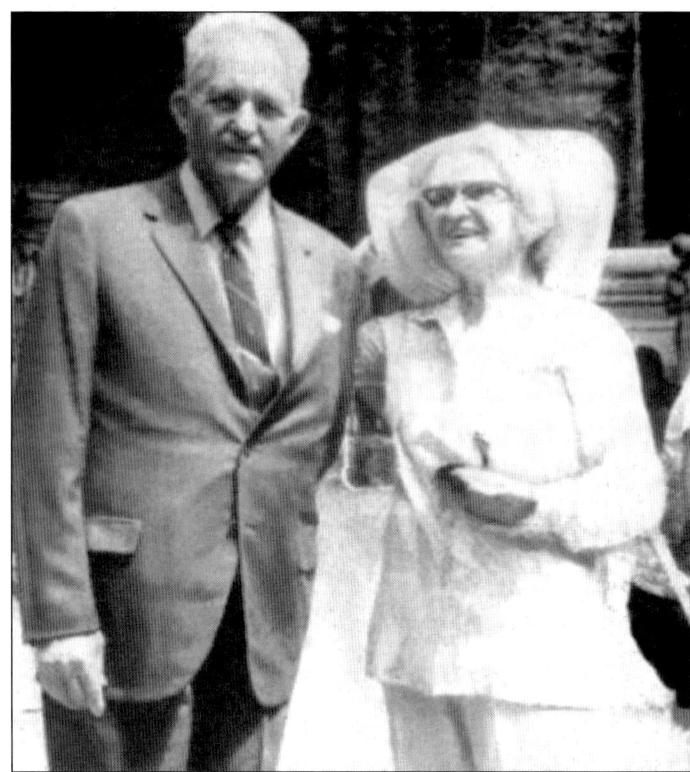

Classmates Louis Abbott and Lena Walker Hicks dressed to the nines for the July 17, 1977, homecoming festivities. Hicks flew in from Florida, and Abbott flew in from California for the celebration. Hicks said, "Why, we'd fly from the moon to get here." (Courtesy Great Smoky Mountains National Park archives.)

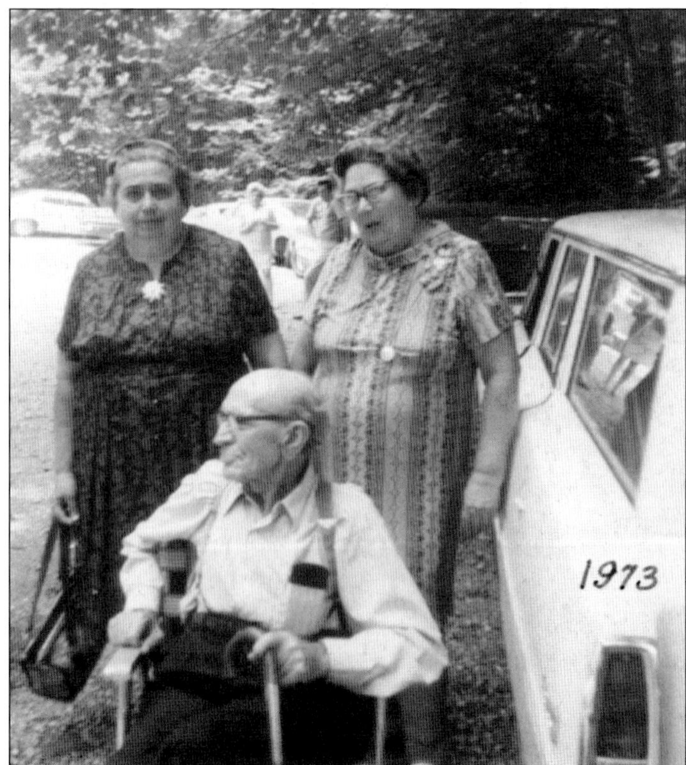

Effie Phipps (left) and Hazel Hembree (right) are pictured with their father, noted area photographer Jim Shelton, at the July 15, 1973, homecoming. (Courtesy Great Smoky Mountains National Park archives.)

Jim Shelton, the photographer of Little Greenbrier, talks with a guest at the July 15, 1973, homecoming picnic. Jim's wife, Sarah Caroline, passed away in 1966. (Courtesy Great Smoky Mountains National Park archives.)

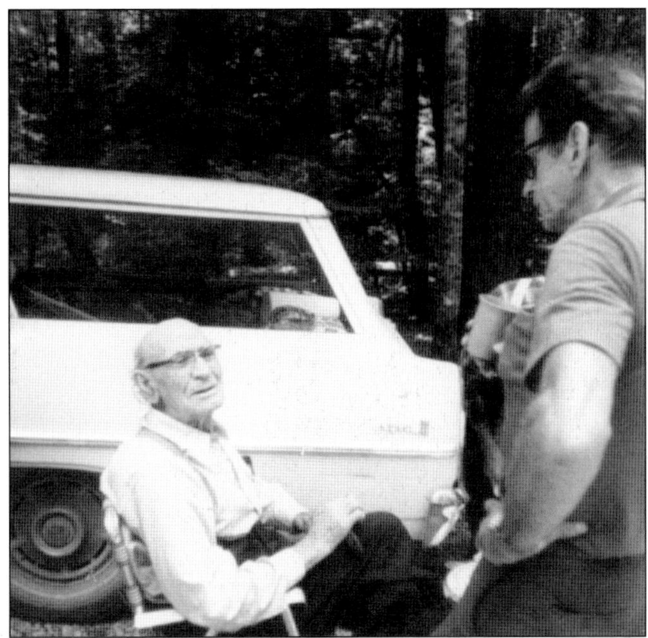

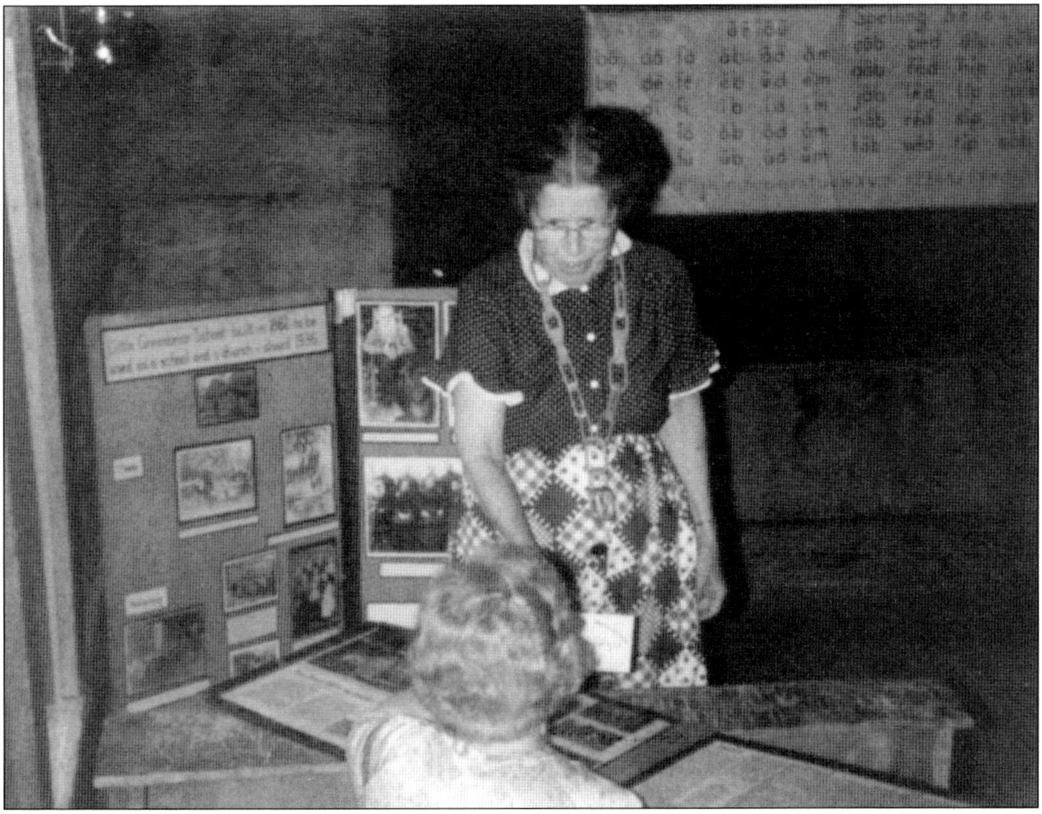

Margaret "Miss Elsie" Burrell set up this display of memorabilia at a homecoming event. She is usually in period outfits, so this is a rare image of her at the school in everyday clothing. (Courtesy Great Smoky Mountains National Park archives.)

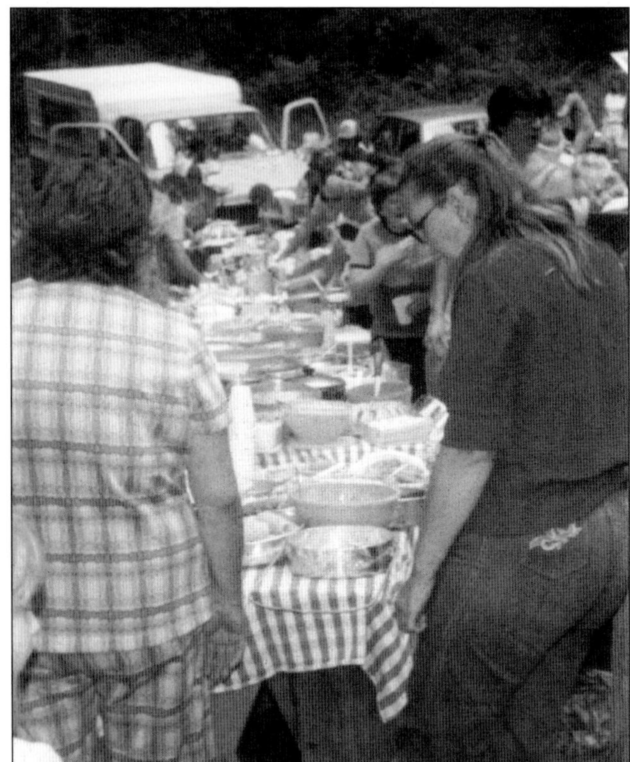

Food is never in short supply at any homecoming event, and several picnic tables are brought in for the day. (Courtesy Great Smoky Mountains National Park archives.)

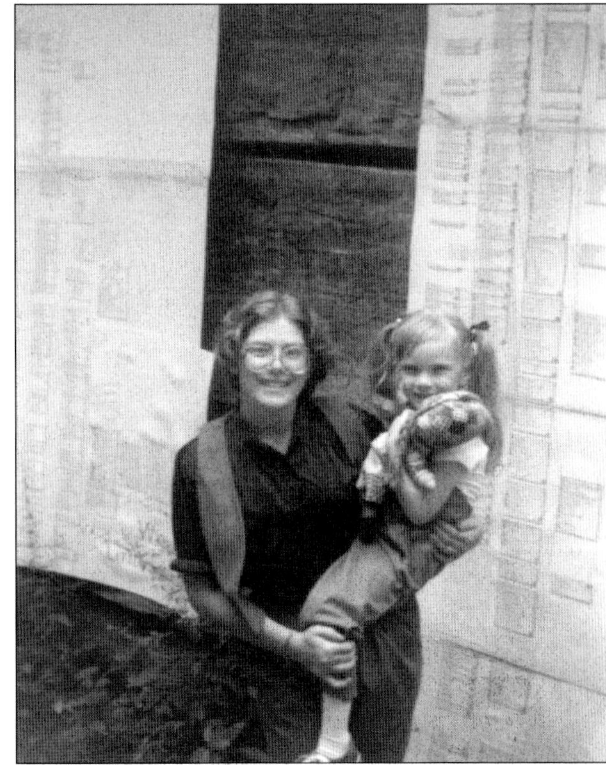

Two girls stand in front of family/genealogy charts on display at a homecoming. For participants at the homecomings, genealogy charts are a godsend for research. (Courtesy Great Smoky Mountains National Park archives.)

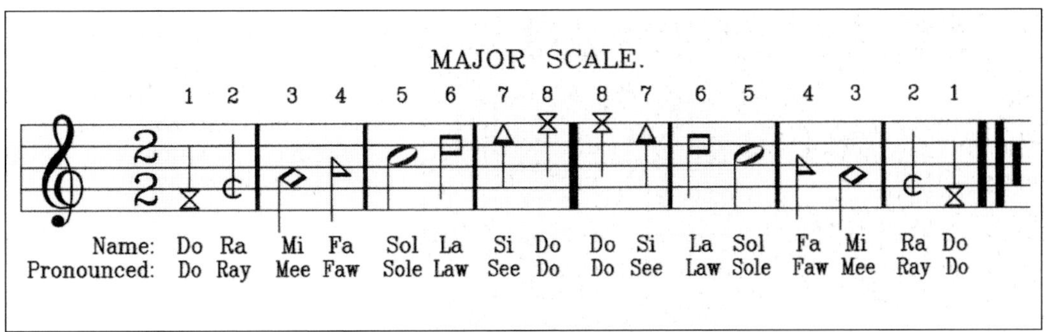

Different shapes correlate to musical notes. This is a major scale starting on "F." (Courtesy oldharp.org.)

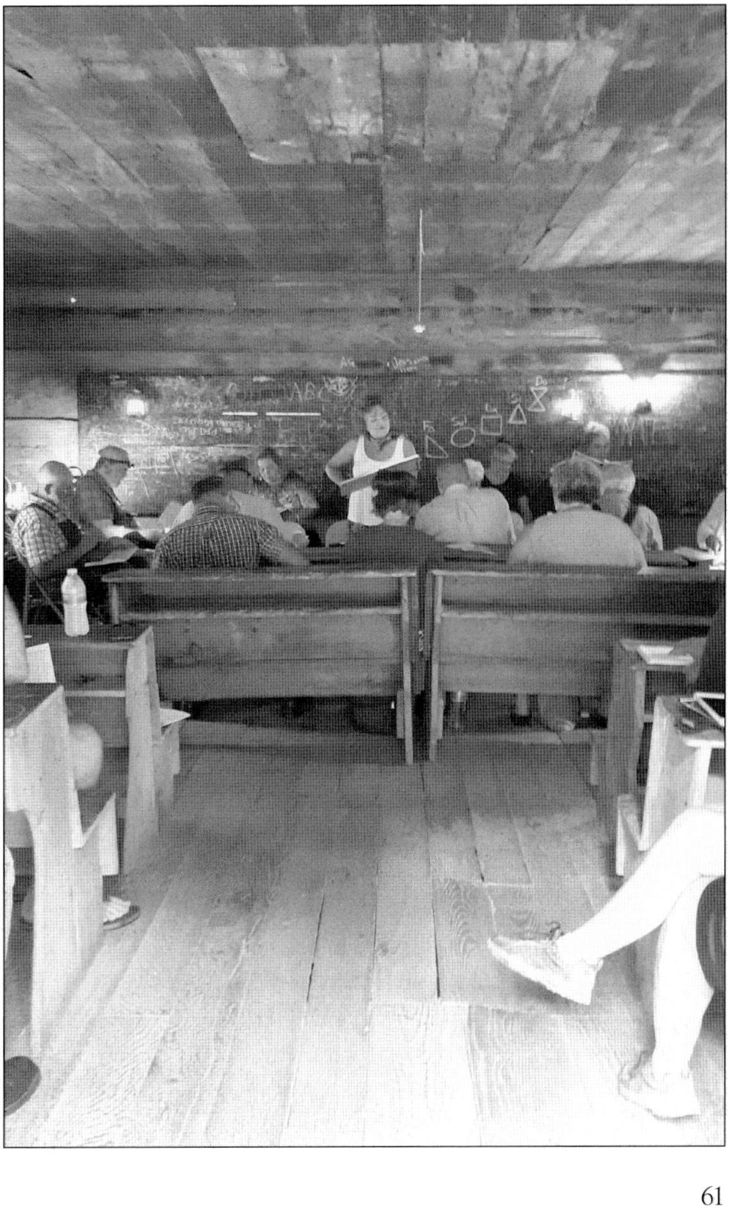

Tina Becker, alto, is shown leading a song at the 2019 singing at the Little Greenbrier School. The leader of the song picks out their favorites to perform. (Photograph by the author.)

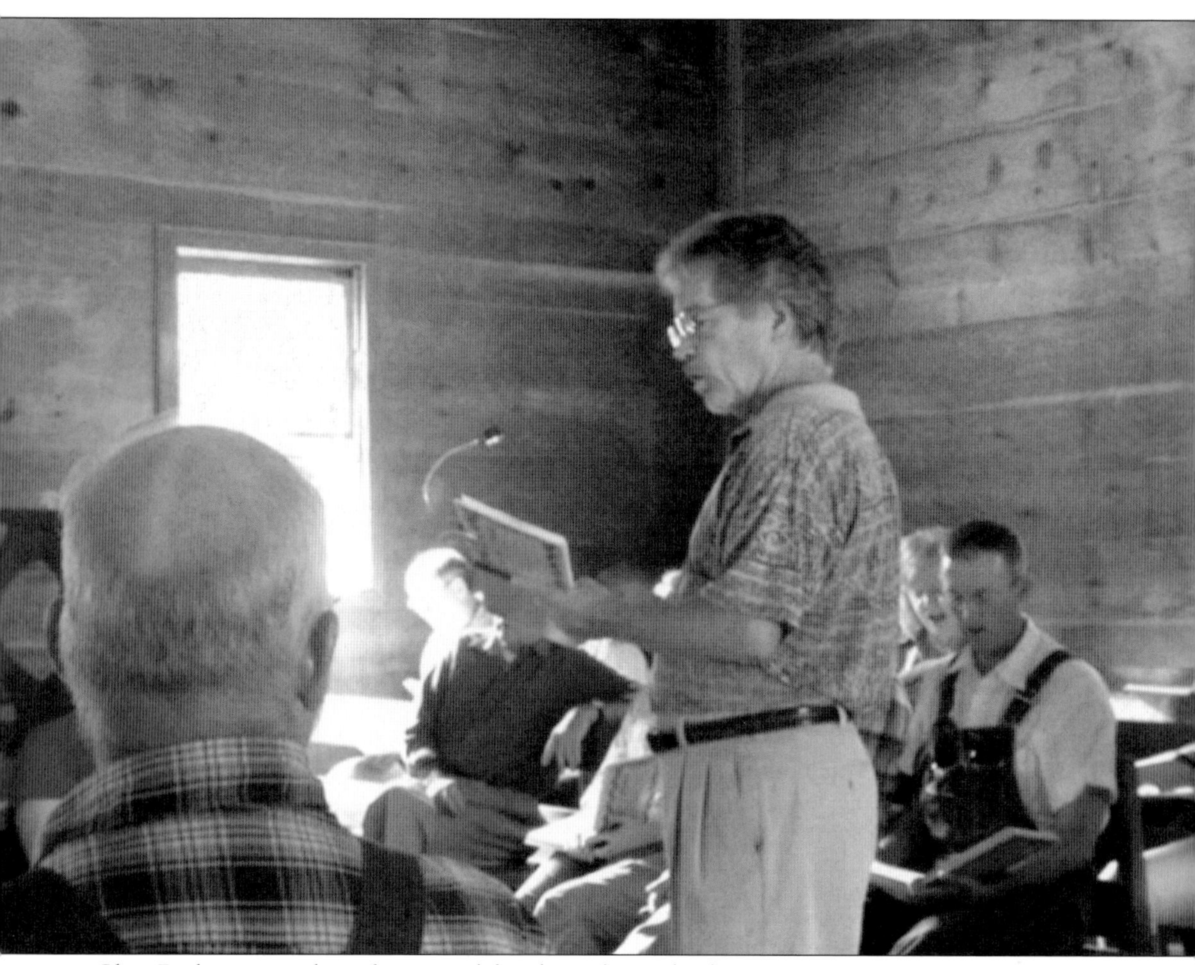

Chaz Barber, a member of a musical family, is shown leading a song on August 18, 2013. Barber became interested in shape-note music when he was attending the University of Tennessee for his master's degree. Participants of a singing take turns leading the song of their choice. (Photograph by Tina Becker.)

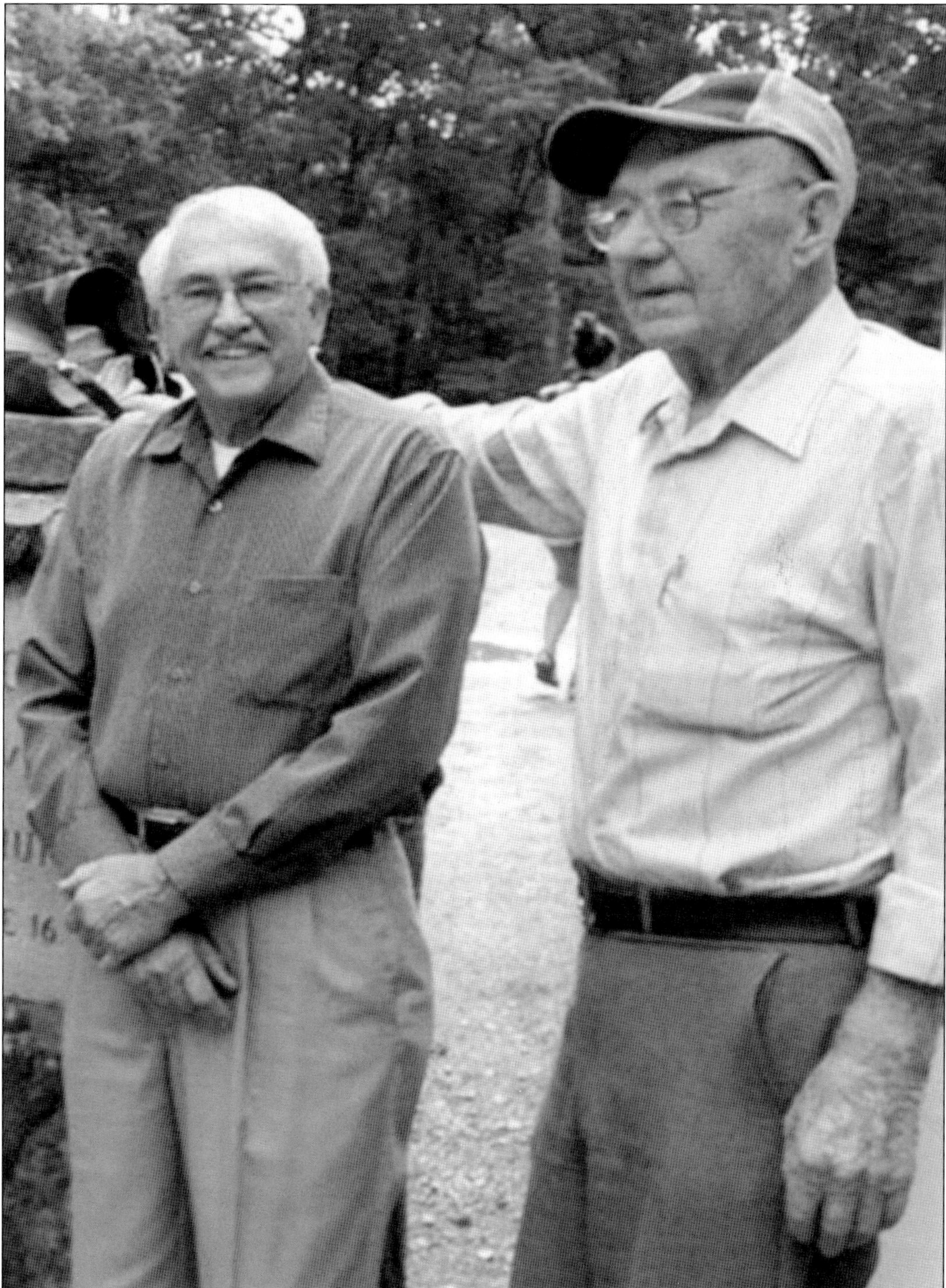

Paul Clabo (left) and Odis Abbott were mainstays at the Little Greenbrier School's singings. Clabo, who has a rich heritage in the mountains, is still alive at the time of this printing. Abbott was born in Cades Cove on November 7, 1919. He passed away on July 14, 2014—the day after a singing at Little Greenbrier School. (Photograph by Tina Becker.)

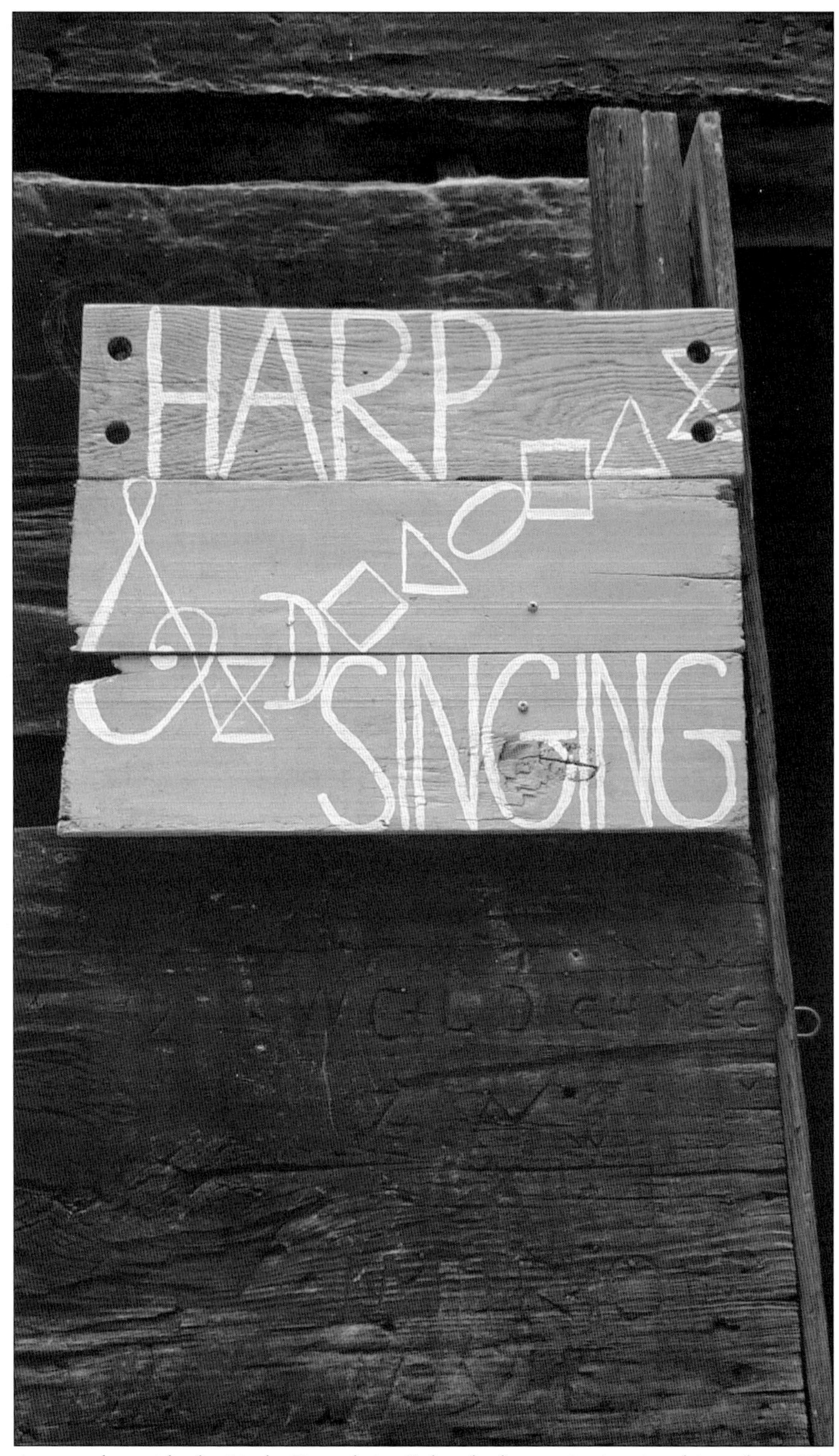

This sign is posted outside the Little Greenbrier School when a singing is taking place. The sign has been spotted at several different singings, not just at Little Greenbrier. (Photograph by the author.)

Six

National Park Era

Margaret Elsie "Miss Elsie" Burrell was a retired educator from Maryville, Tennessee, and was best friends with the Walker sisters from Little Greenbrier. She was very familiar with the area and felt the need to educate visitors to the park about the community. She developed a curriculum, presented it to the National Park Service, and got it approved for use as an interpretative program at the Little Greenbrier School. Her original curriculum is still followed today. Burrell's interpretive program started on a Tuesday in June 1970. The program has run continuously since then, except during the COVID-19 pandemic shutdown in 2020 and 2021. It is the longest running program in Great Smoky Mountains National Park.

Robin "Miss Robin" Goddard was a neighbor of Miss Elsie and was introduced to the Walker sisters at an early age. She spent several weeks each year at the Walker home from age four through high school. While she was there, she would help with the day-to-day chores—carding wool, making sauerkraut, frying pies, keeping house, and others.

As Miss Elsie aged and could not keep up with the weekly programs, Miss Robin helped her and eventually assumed sole responsibility for the weekly seasonal interpretive program.

Never giving the exact same program twice, Miss Robin covers the history of the building and how it was made, detailed information about local families (including the Walker family), and other local topics, including shape-note singing. If shape-note singing does come up in conversation, Miss Robin will play a selection of that music on her tape player. Depending on the audience, an impromptu spelling bee might also be held.

For programs, the school is decorated with several period items: bonnets, tools, samplers, bells, Blue Back Spellers, McGuffey readers, baskets, charts, and toys.

Many visitors come back repeatedly, sometimes several times a year. They enjoy the program, hiking, exploring the cemetery, and conversation with Miss Robin. Many visitors return around the same time every year and have been coming to the school for long enough that they remember Miss Robin and address her by name. The volunteers likewise recognize the faces of many repeat visitors and also know their names. Sometimes, the weekly programs almost take on the semblance of a family reunion.

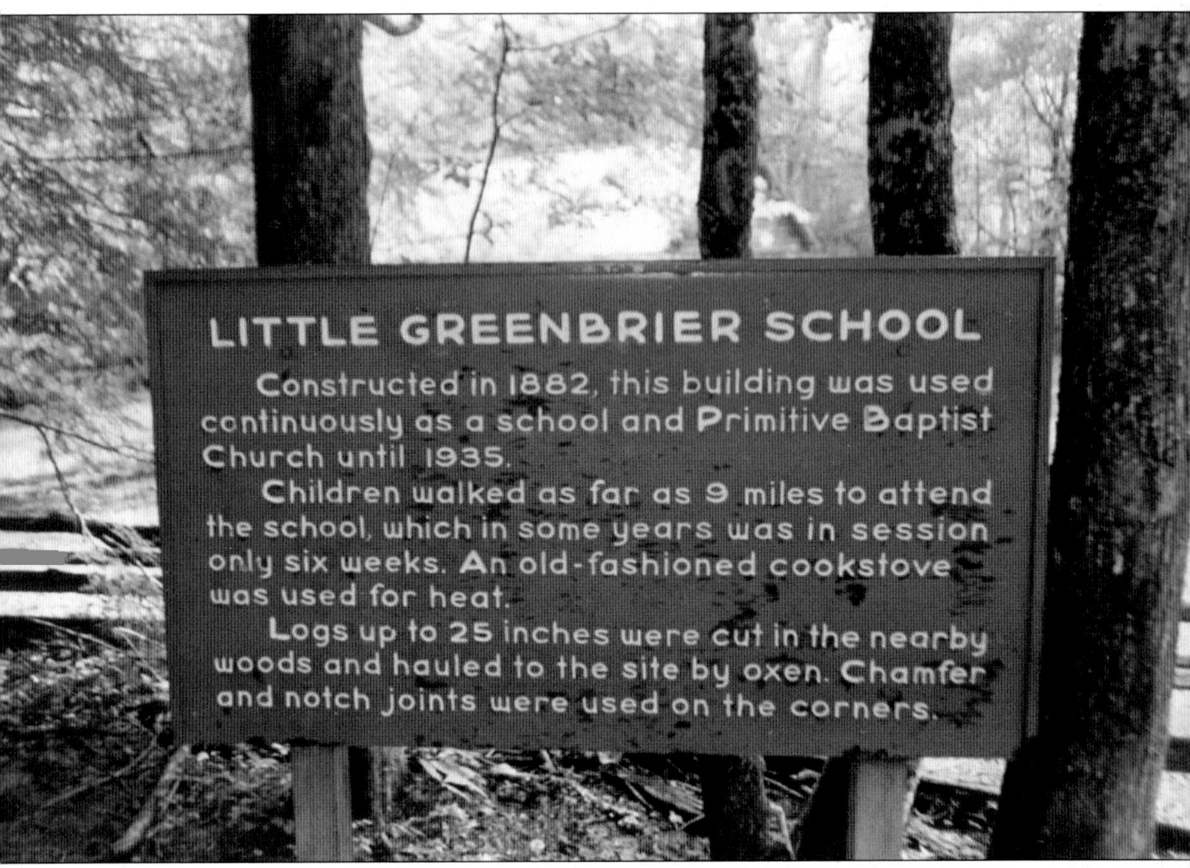

This sign stood outside the school for many years in several different places. It is pictured here in 1989. (Courtesy Great Smoky Mountains National Park archives.)

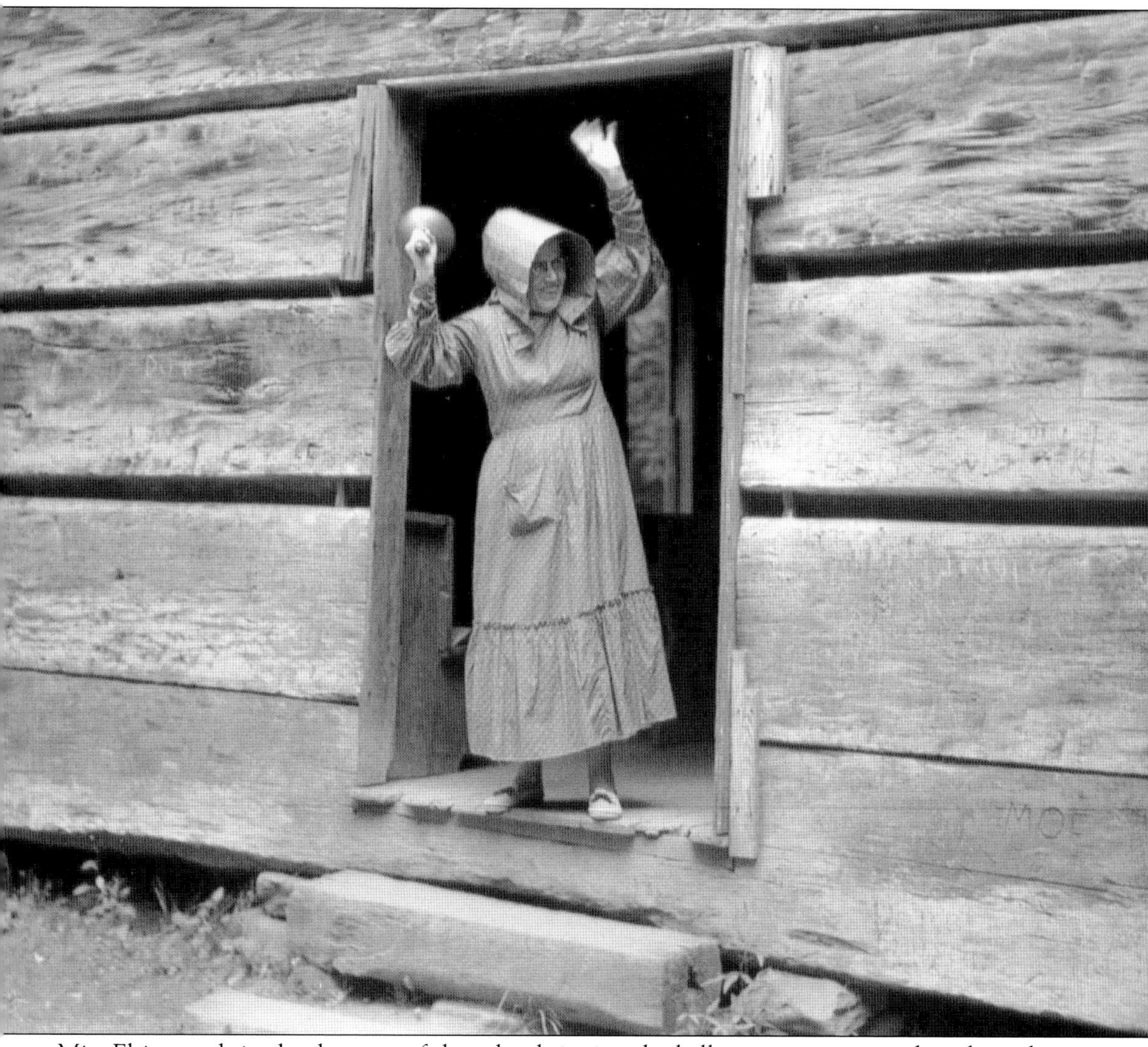

Miss Elsie stands in the doorway of the school ringing the bell as a group approaches along the trail on July 23, 1974. Miss Elsie's programs began in June 1970 and were held weekly from April through October. The program has continued with Miss Robin taking over for Miss Elsie. The only exceptions to date have been during the summers of 2020 and 2021 due to the COVID-19 pandemic. (Courtesy Great Smoky Mountains National Park archives.)

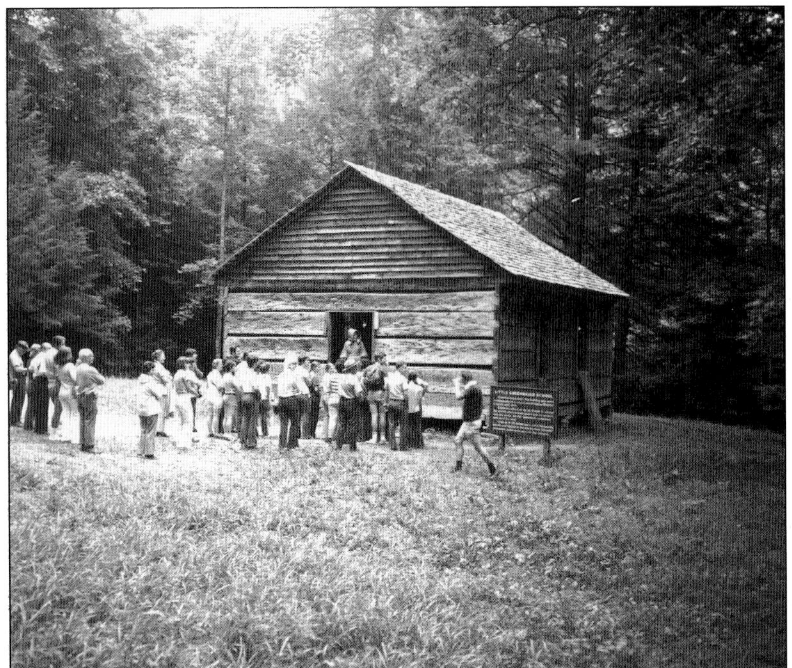

Students and visitors assemble at the entry to the school on July 23, 1974. Miss Elsie is looking toward the trail for any stragglers. (Courtesy Great Smoky Mountains National Park archives.)

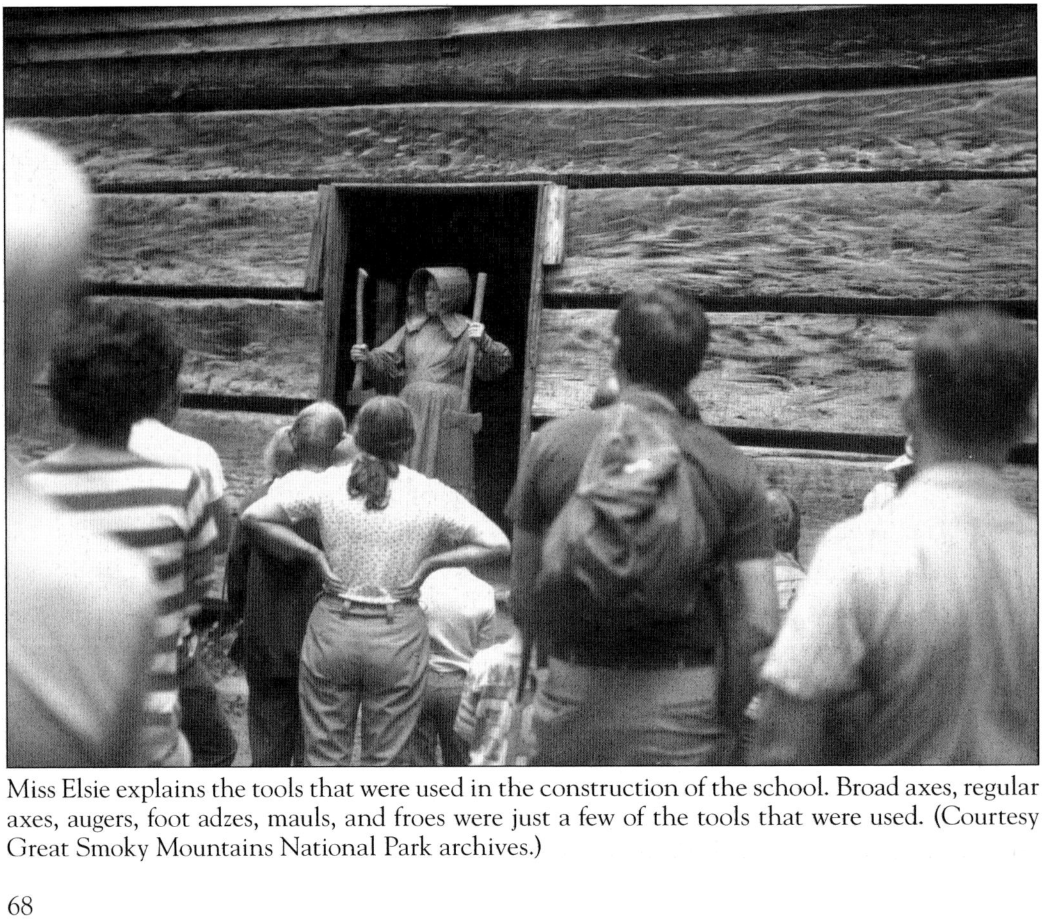

Miss Elsie explains the tools that were used in the construction of the school. Broad axes, regular axes, augers, foot adzes, mauls, and froes were just a few of the tools that were used. (Courtesy Great Smoky Mountains National Park archives.)

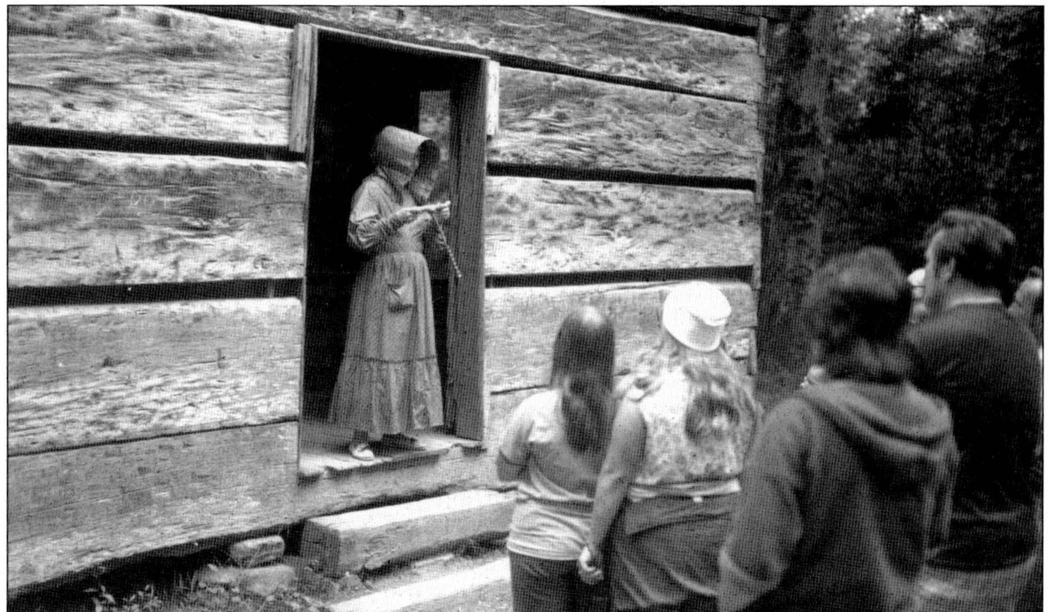

Miss Elsie explains how the auger was used in the construction of the school. Holes were made through the logs next to where the door was being cut, and dogwood branches were placed in the holes to keep the logs plumb. The same dogwood branches that were placed in the school in 1881 remain there today. Note that the logs were not chinked, but boards were nailed to the inside of the school's walls to prevent wind and weather from coming in. (Courtesy Great Smoky Mountains National Park archives.)

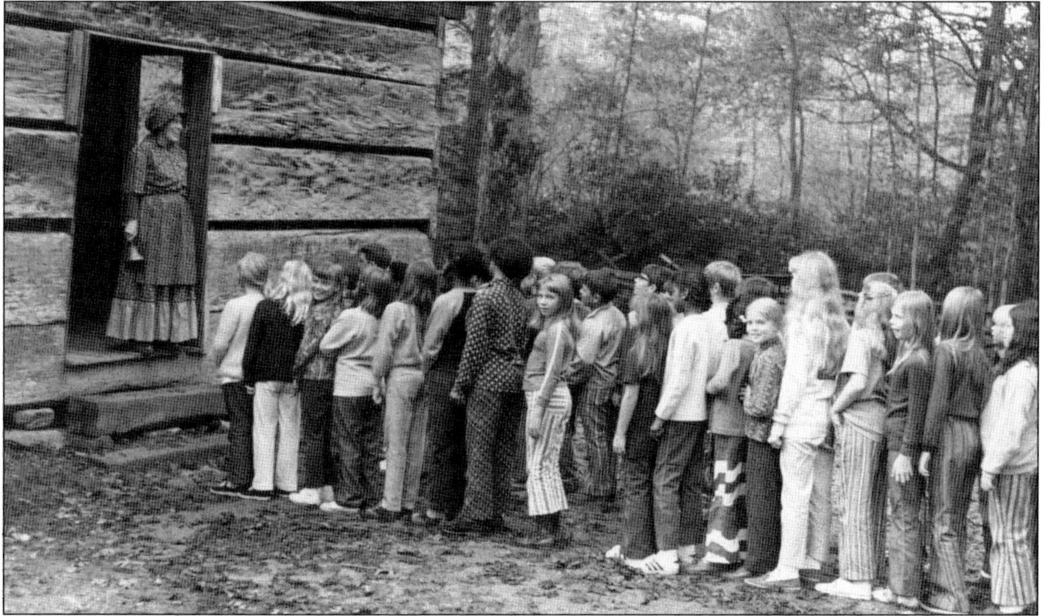

After initial introductions and getting the attention of the crowd of schoolchildren, Miss Elsie lined them up to enter the school. Thanks to her experience working as an educator for many years, Miss Elsie was never at a loss when it came to how to handle students. (Courtesy Great Smoky Mountains National Park archives.)

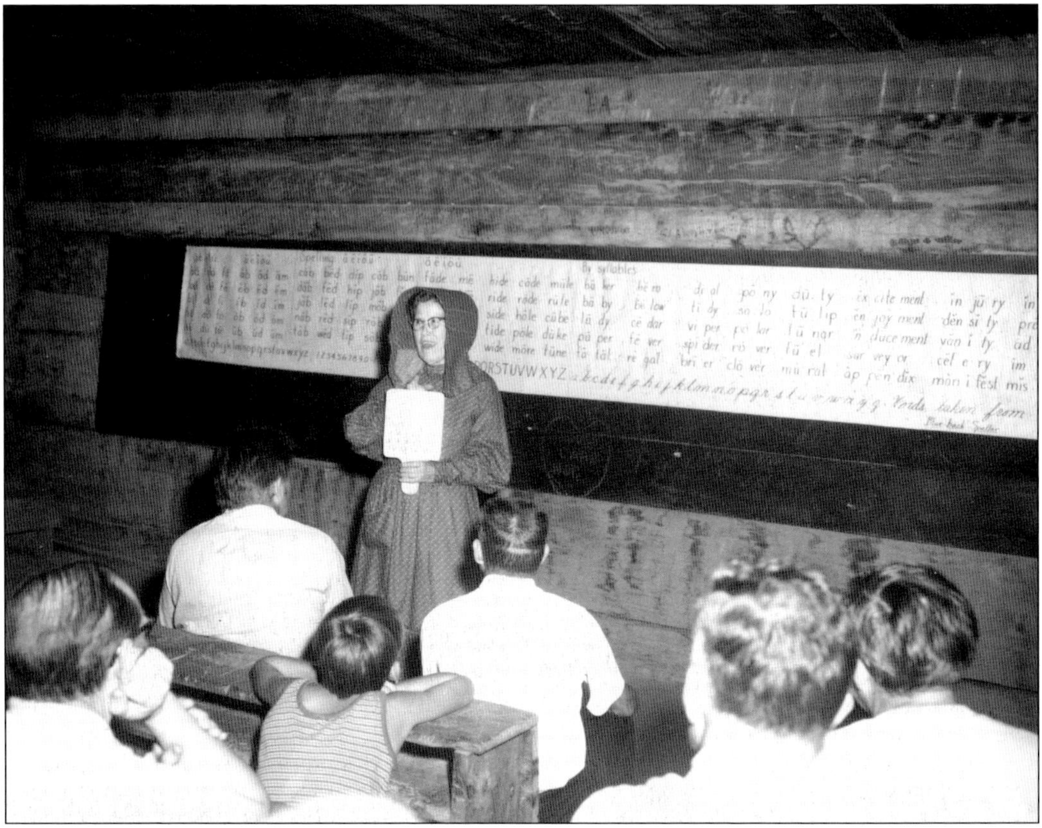

"The boys sit on my left side; the girls on my right," said Miss Elsie. On the wall behind her is a chart of words taken from Webster's Blue Back Speller. Words are separated into syllables, and vowels are marked to indicate proper pronunciation. These paper charts were used weekly until the mid-2010s, when they were replaced with plastic-coated canvas charts. (Courtesy Great Smoky Mountains National Park archives.)

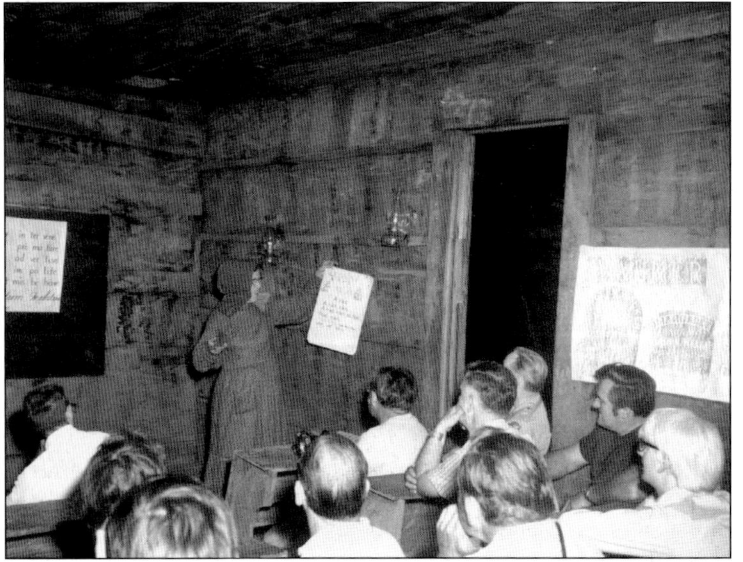

Miss Elsie entertained visitors during her programs. Note the lanterns on the wall, which were filled with coal oil when this photograph was taken on July 23, 1974. Note that the men were on Miss Elsie's left. (Courtesy Great Smoky Mountains National Park archives.)

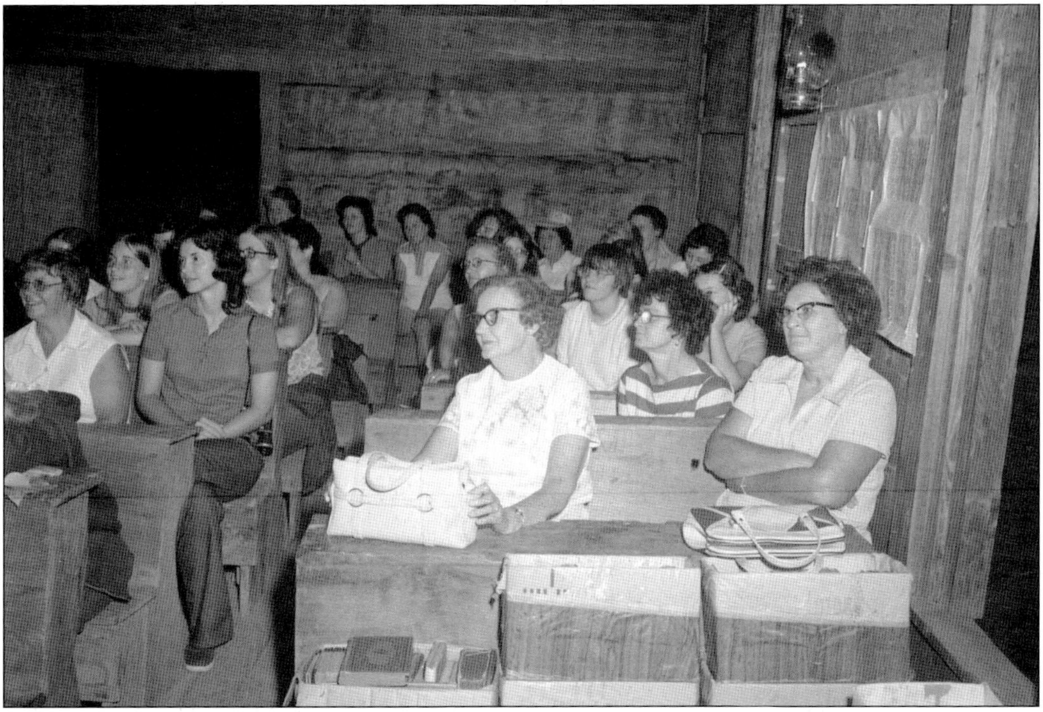

The women are on the right for one of Miss Elsie's programs in 1974. Rubbings of the Walker family tombstones are hanging on the wall. (Courtesy Great Smoky Mountains National Park archives.)

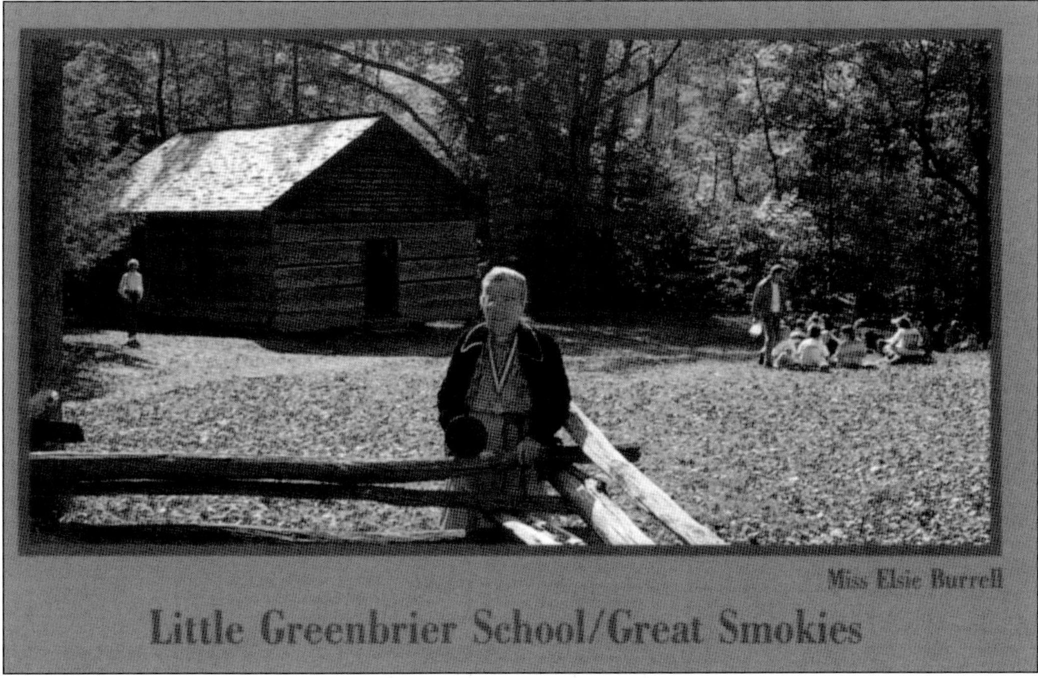

Miss Elsie was so famous that she got her own postcard. Although she was never prideful about her accomplishments, she had too many to properly note them all. (Courtesy Great Smoky Mountains National Park archives.)

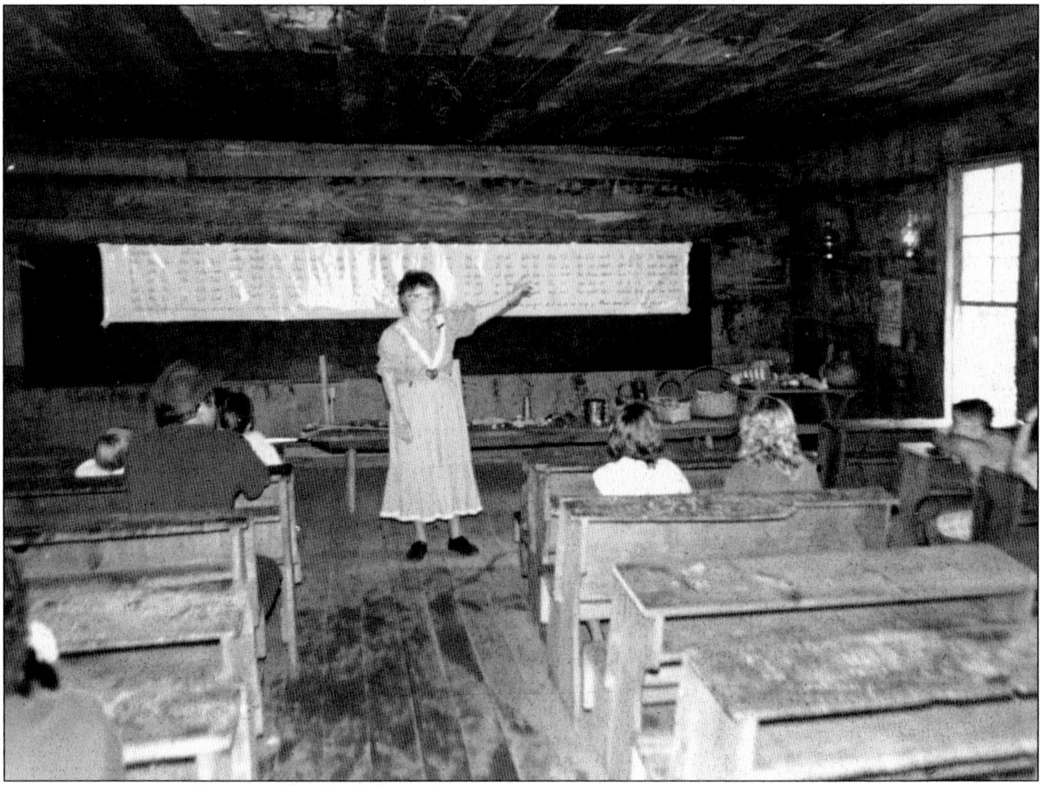

Miss Elsie leads a program for an unusually small group. She would explain how differently spelling was taught then versus how it is taught now. (Courtesy Great Smoky Mountains National Park archives.)

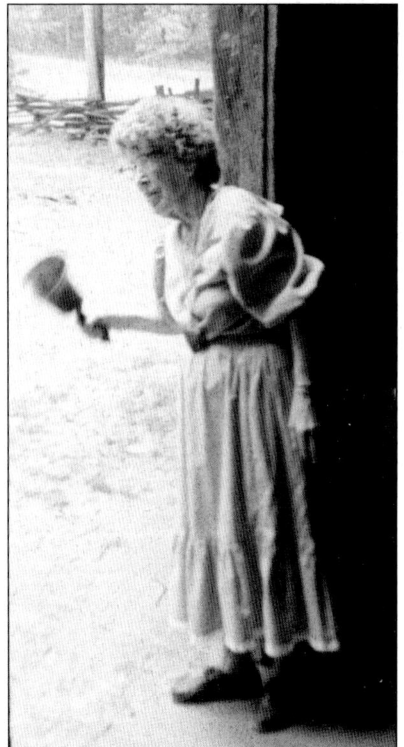

Miss Elsie rings the school bell to let everyone know that the program would be starting soon. (Courtesy Great Smoky Mountains National Park archives.)

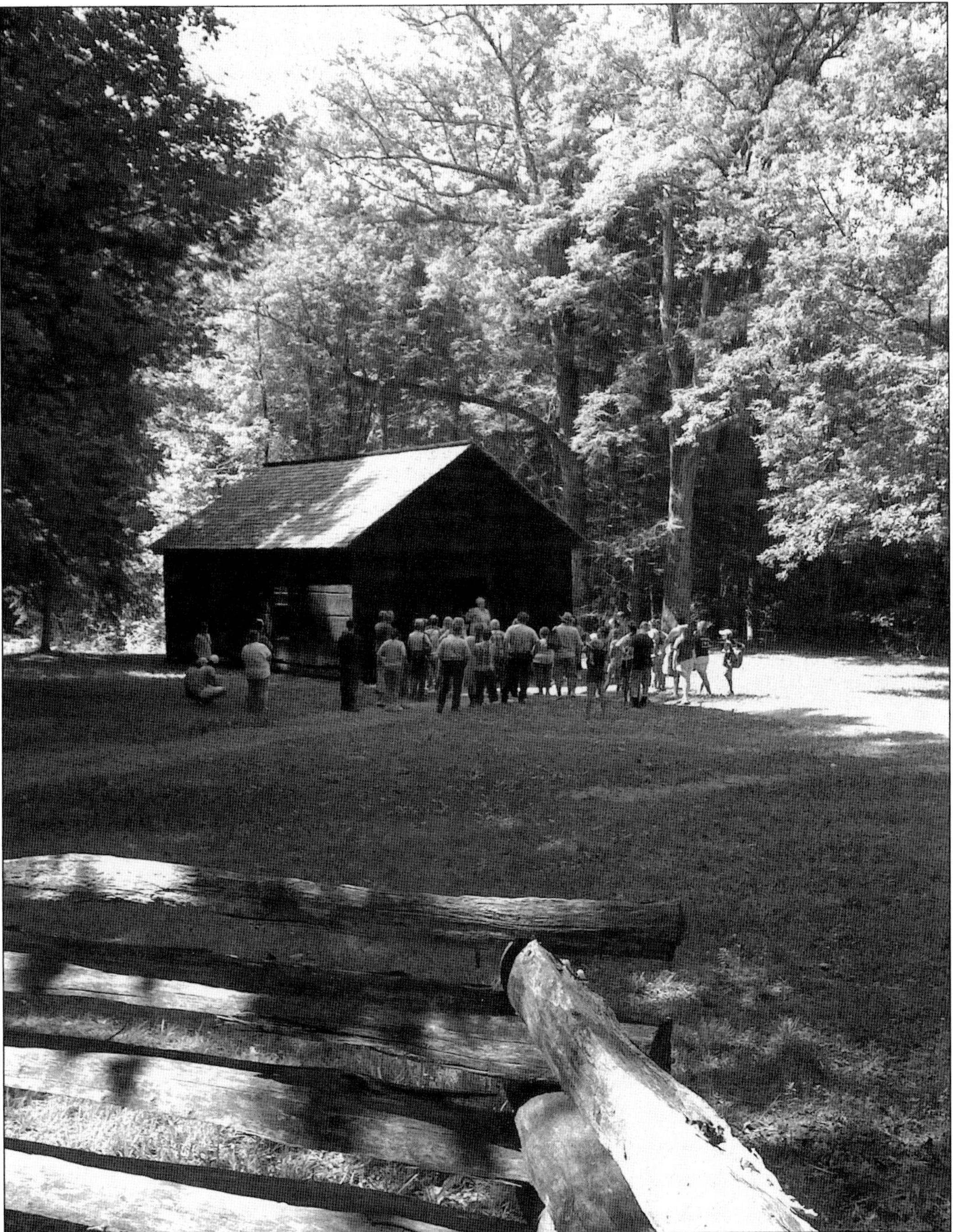

Crowds of visitors often number in the hundreds each Tuesday during tourist season. Here, Miss Robin starts the program with a tool explanation and a description of how the building was constructed. (Photograph by the author.)

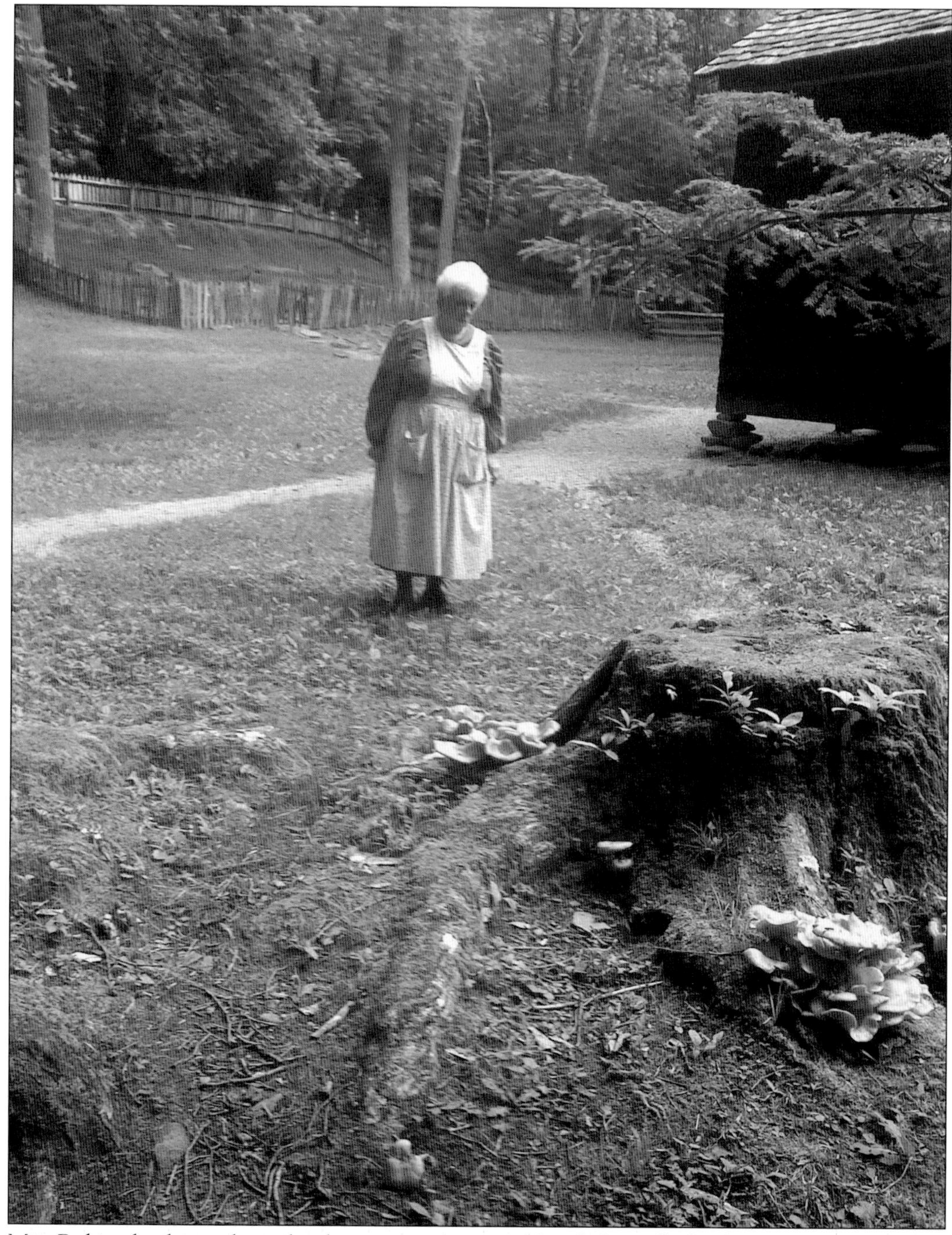

Miss Robin checks on the jack-o-lantern mushrooms (*Omphalotus illudens*) that appear each year around the tree stumps at the Little Greenbrier School. (Photograph by the author.)

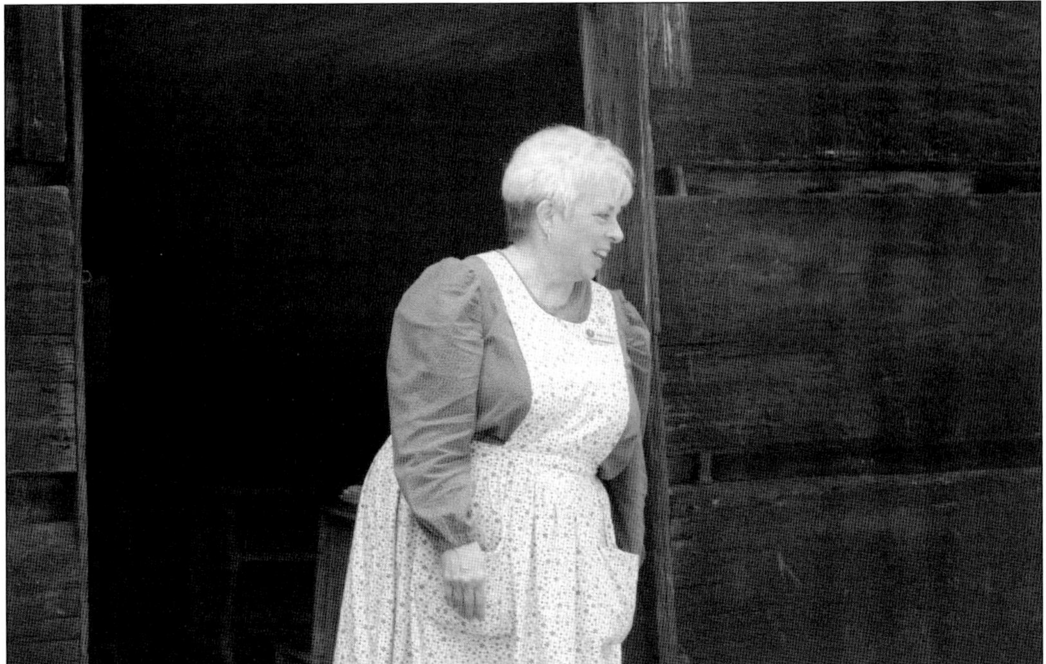

Miss Robin stands outside the Little Greenbrier School before one of her programs in 2019. With the longest-running program presented in the park, the school draws crowds that can number in the thousands by season's end. (Photograph by the author.)

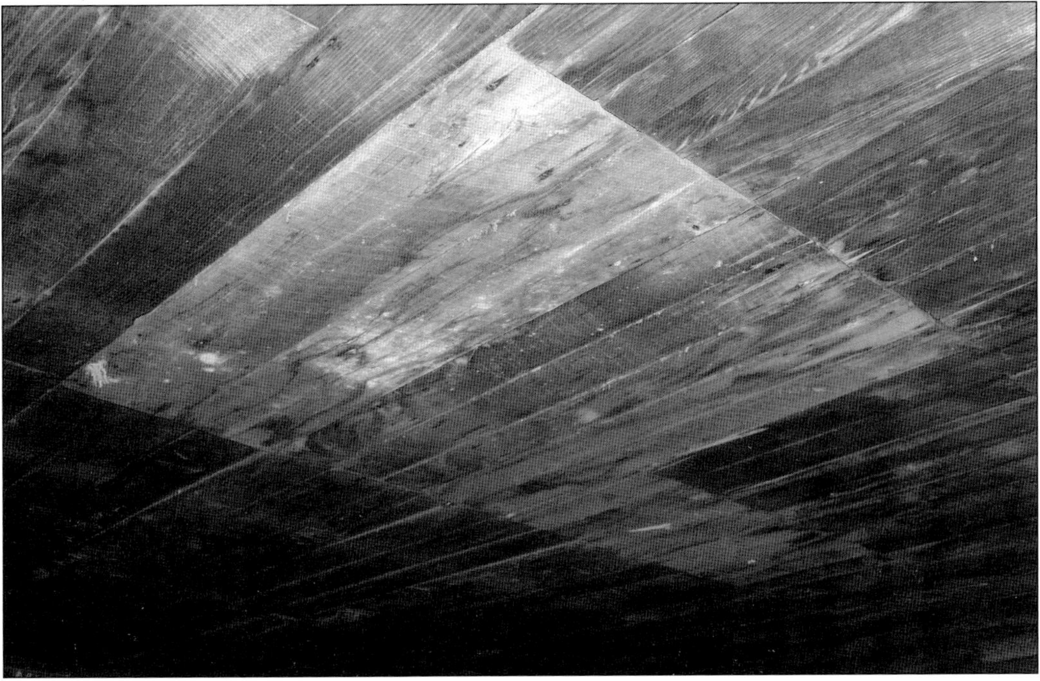

When the stove was removed from the schoolhouse, an L-shaped replacement of the ceiling boards was installed. This is in the middle of the school, where the stove's piping and flue once went out through the roof. (Photograph by the author.)

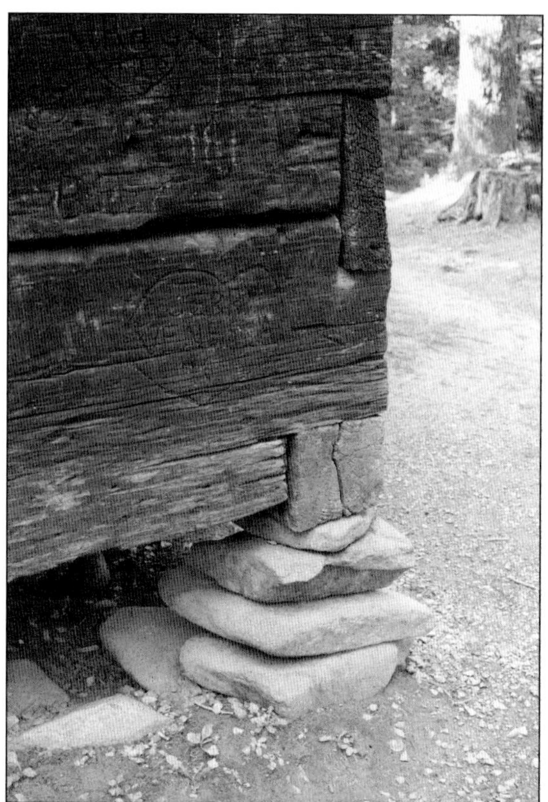

Even though the stones have changed over the years, the basic principle of them being the foundation of the school has not. This bottom log was replaced in the 2010s due to deterioration from flooding in 1993. (Photograph by the author.)

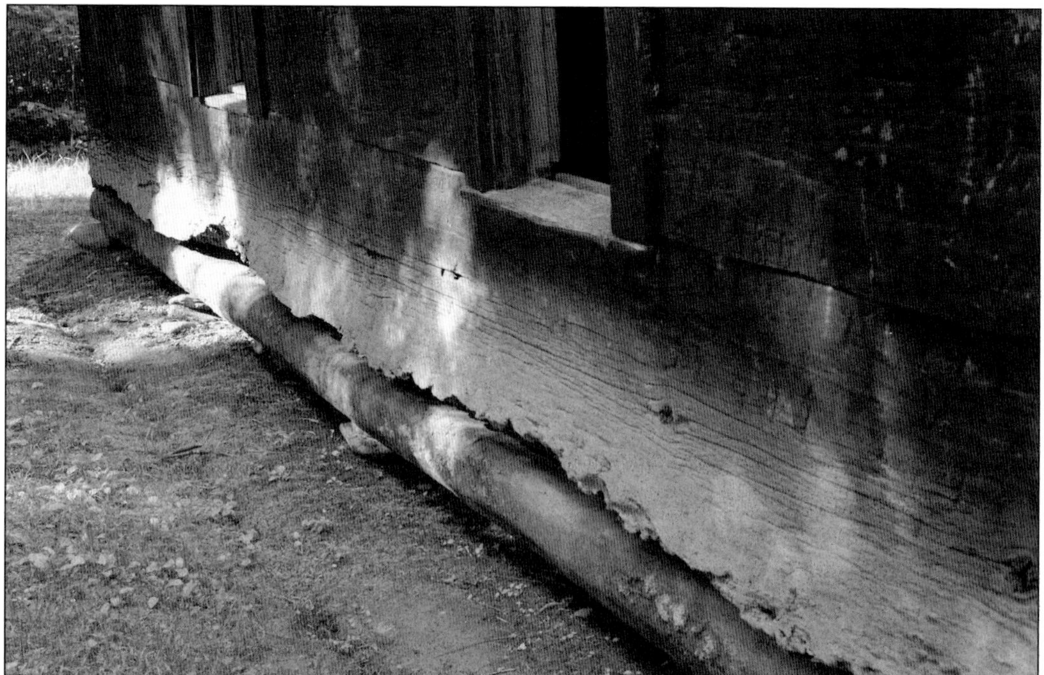

On the opposite side of the school, the bottom log still needs to be replaced. The line from the 1993 flood is visible. (Photograph by the author.)

Seven

Little Greenbrier Cemetery

The cemetery is to the north, close to the building on a sloped lot. Gilbert Abbott's father was visiting his son in 1881 when he suddenly died. He was the first person to be buried at the cemetery and is interred in the upper right corner. He has no tombstone.

There are 59 graves in the cemetery, 39 of which were once marked. Over the years, people have knocked over, stolen, and moved stones; now, not all of them are marked.

In her pamphlet "Rememberin' The Little Greenbriar School and Primitive Baptist Church," Mary Stinnett Crabtree writes, "Shirden Moore and his son Wayne made the pickets for the original fence in 1952. They were made of yellow pine, hauled out of the woods by sled and took to the road where they were loaded on a truck and took to the school house. The original fence was destroyed by vandals who burned the pickets for firewood."

The National Park Service replaced the fencing but was not entirely correct in its placement. In 2016, a dowser identified plots of at least three bodies outside the fence and toward the schoolhouse. The cemetery remains one of the most popular places to visit at the Little Greenbrier School.

The cemetery is considered "dead," meaning that no more burials will occur there. There are still "live" cemeteries in the park where a person may be buried if their family can show a direct connection to the park, such as being born or raised there. The NPS was contacted by Margaret "Miss Elsie" Burrell in the 1970s about families wishing to put modern stones in the cemetery. The NPS agreed to the request as long as the monument was not a "monstrosity," and such an action took place after 1977.

Visitors note that the cemetery has many children and infants. There was a saying at the time that if a child could reach the age of seven, they would make it to heaven, meaning they might make it to adulthood. Without medical care and modern medicines, children were at the mercy of infectious diseases, respiratory ailments, and other childhood maladies.

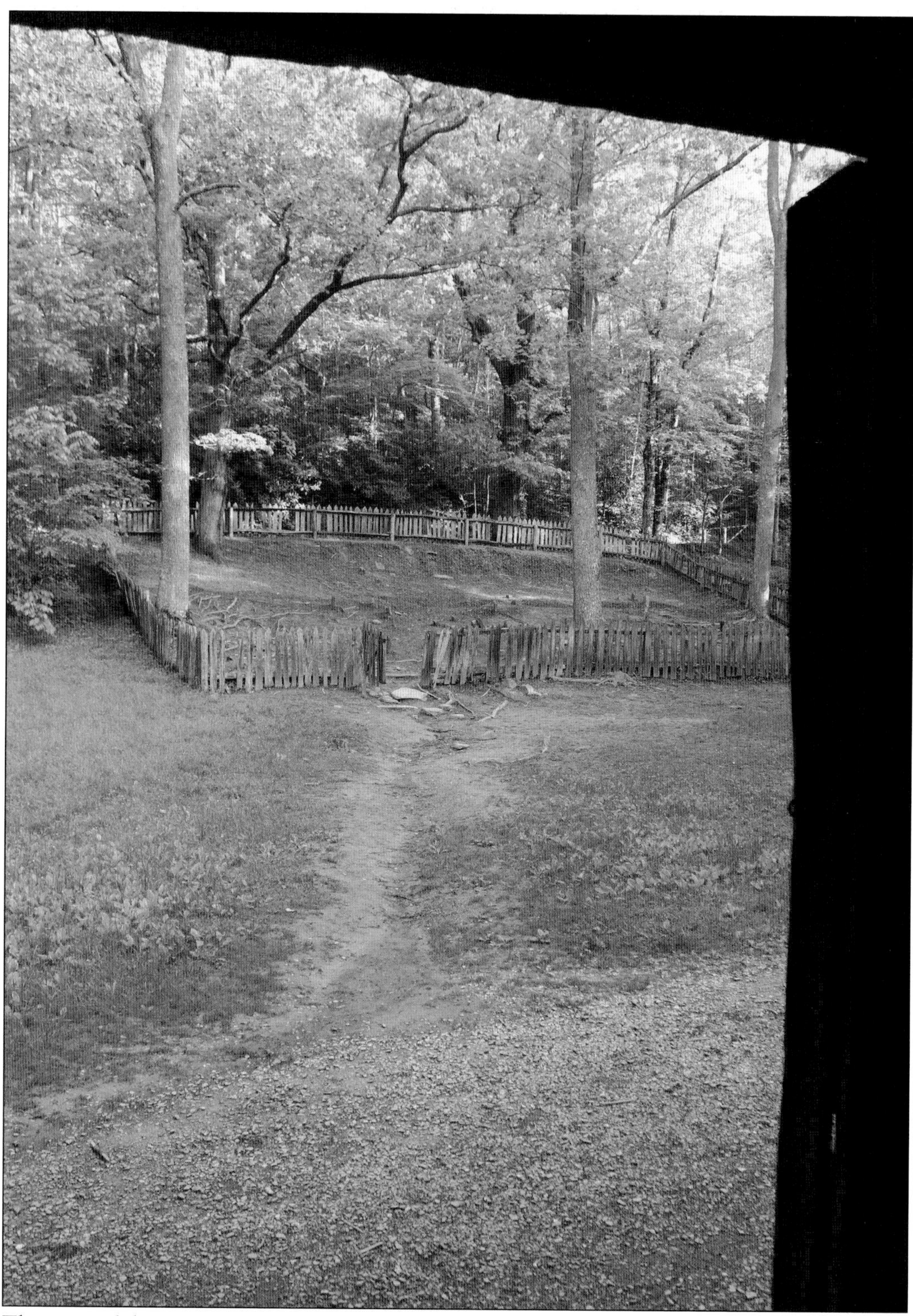

The view of the cemetery from the Little Greenbrier School door is serene. With few modern stones, it may appear empty from a distance. (Photograph by the author.)

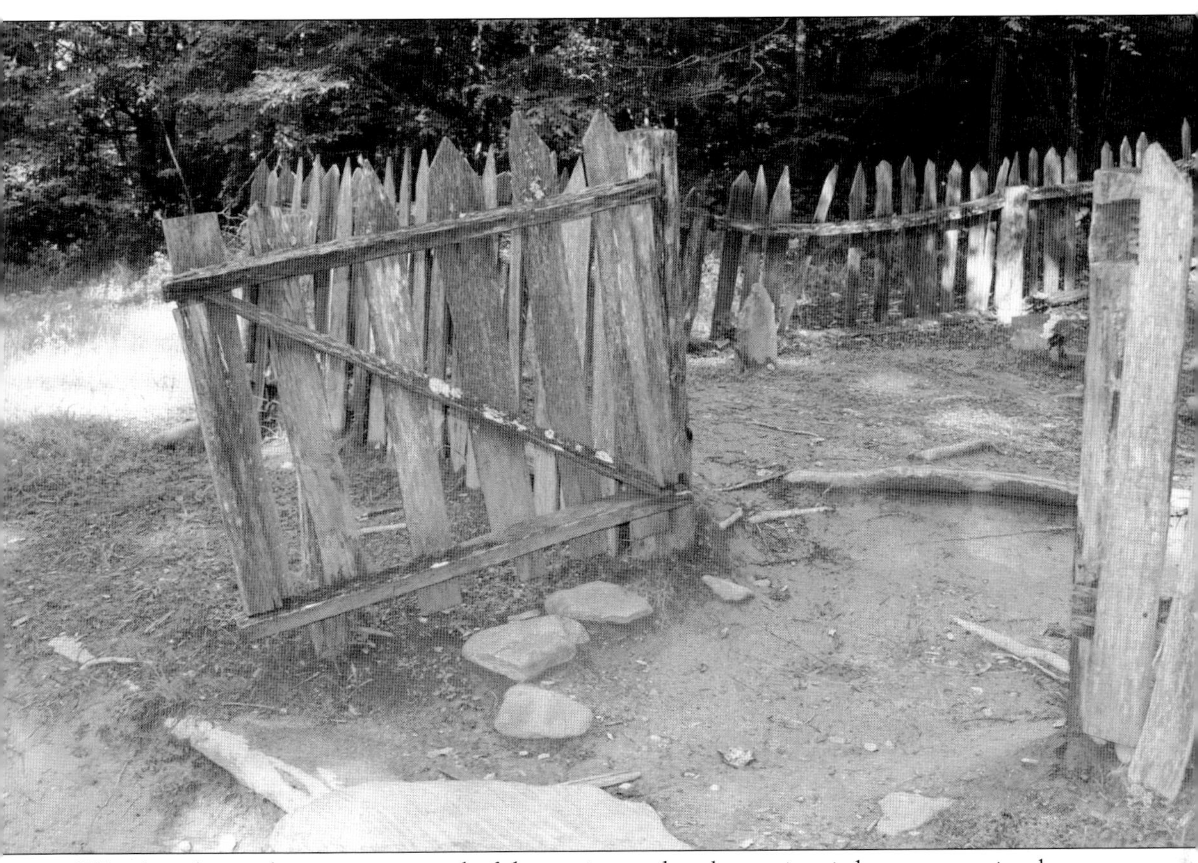

Whether this is the gate to a wonderful eternity or the alternative, it hangs precariously on a hinge. Although the fence is sadly in need of repairs, one can hope for the best in coming years. (Photograph by the author.)

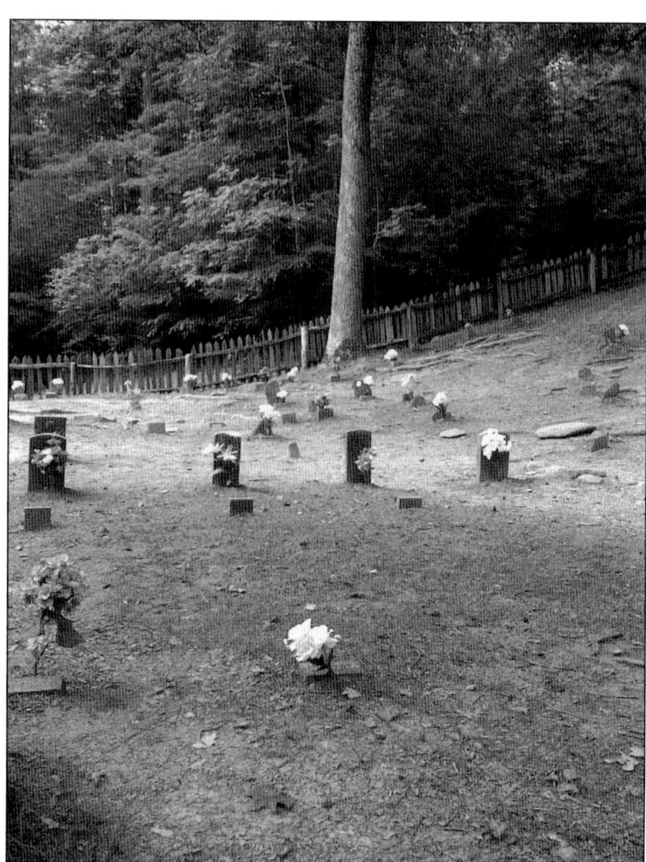

Decoration day at the Little Greenbrier Cemetery is very colorful. Flowers adorn almost all the graves in this photograph from the mid-2010s. (Photograph by the author.)

The most recent gravestone in the cemetery belongs to Peggy Stinnett Hicks. It is very modest—definitely not a "monstrosity," as the National Park Service requested when they gave permission for modern stones to be included in the cemetery. The top was knocked off its base several years ago and still awaits repair. (Photograph by the author.)

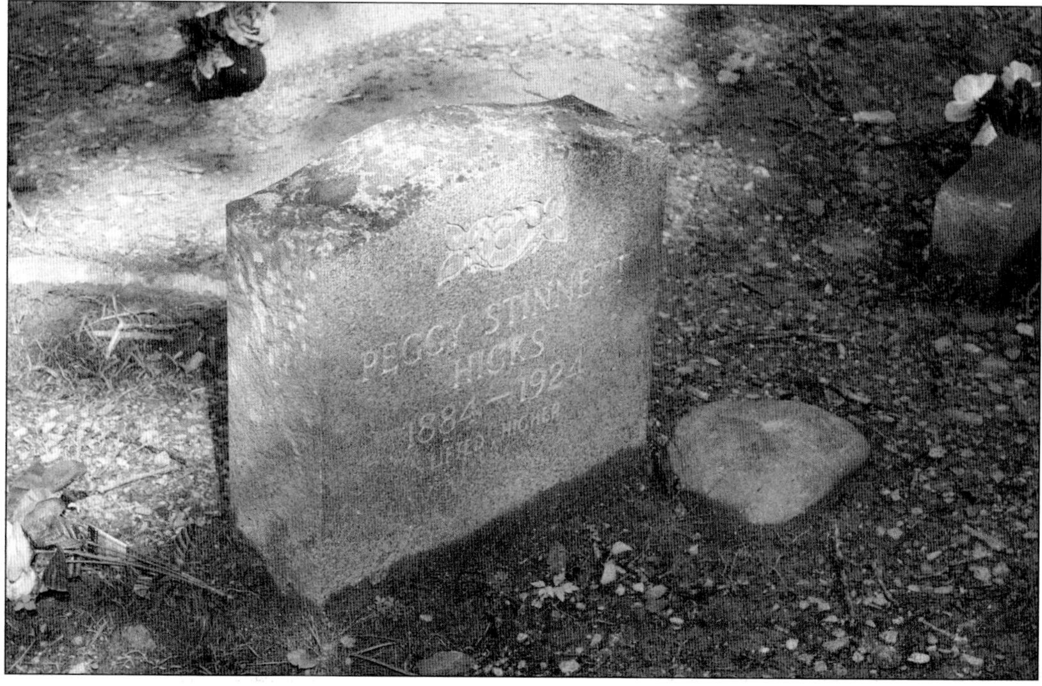

Some fieldstone markers have been replaced with modern stones. The cemetery is quite worn from constant visitation, and has little grass. (Photograph by the author.)

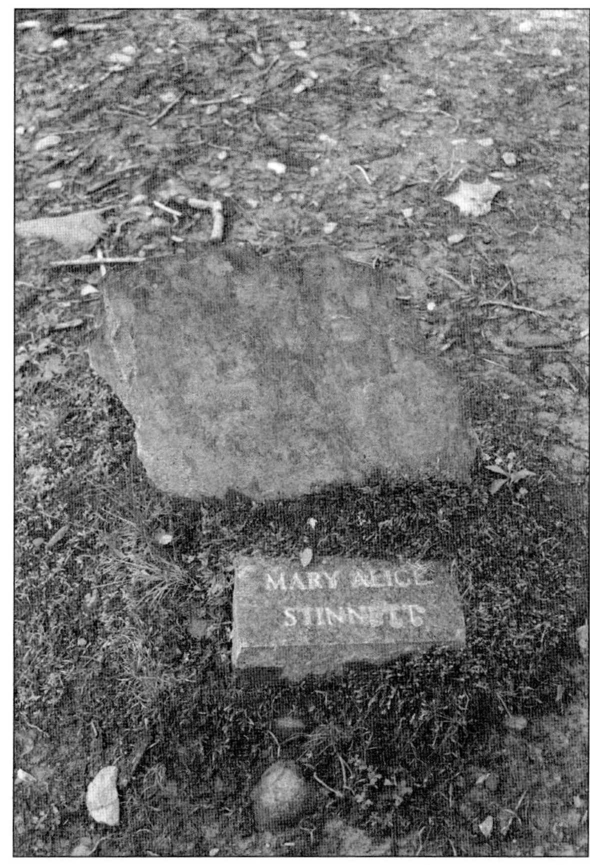

This is the view of the Little Greenbrier School from the top of the cemetery. The original fencing, also called paling, was put up in the 1950s. (Photograph by the author.)

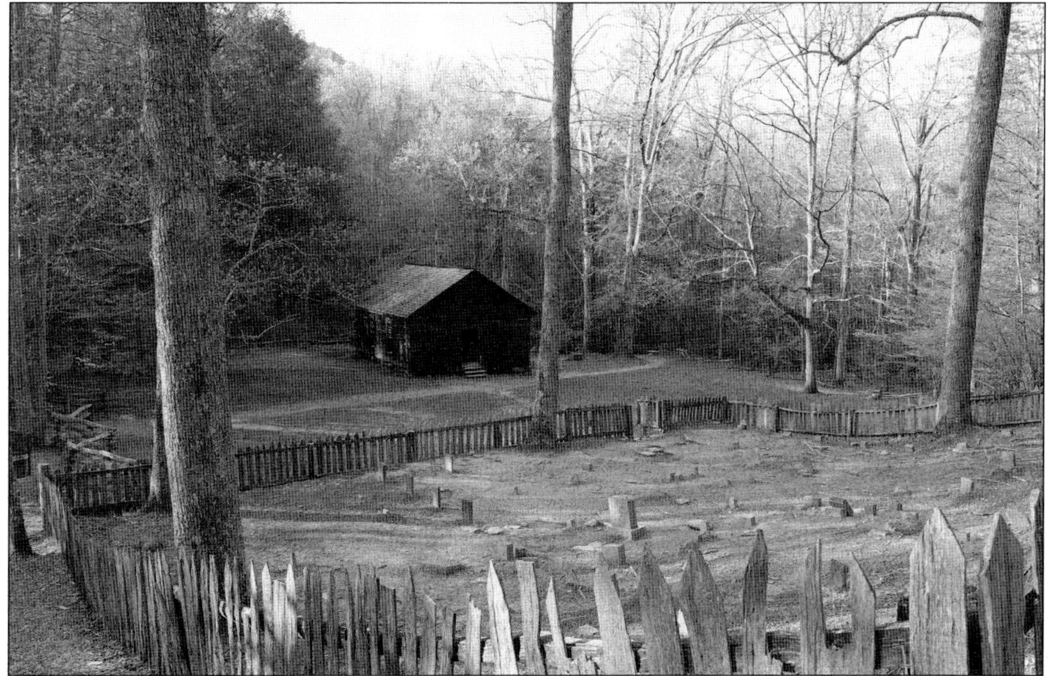

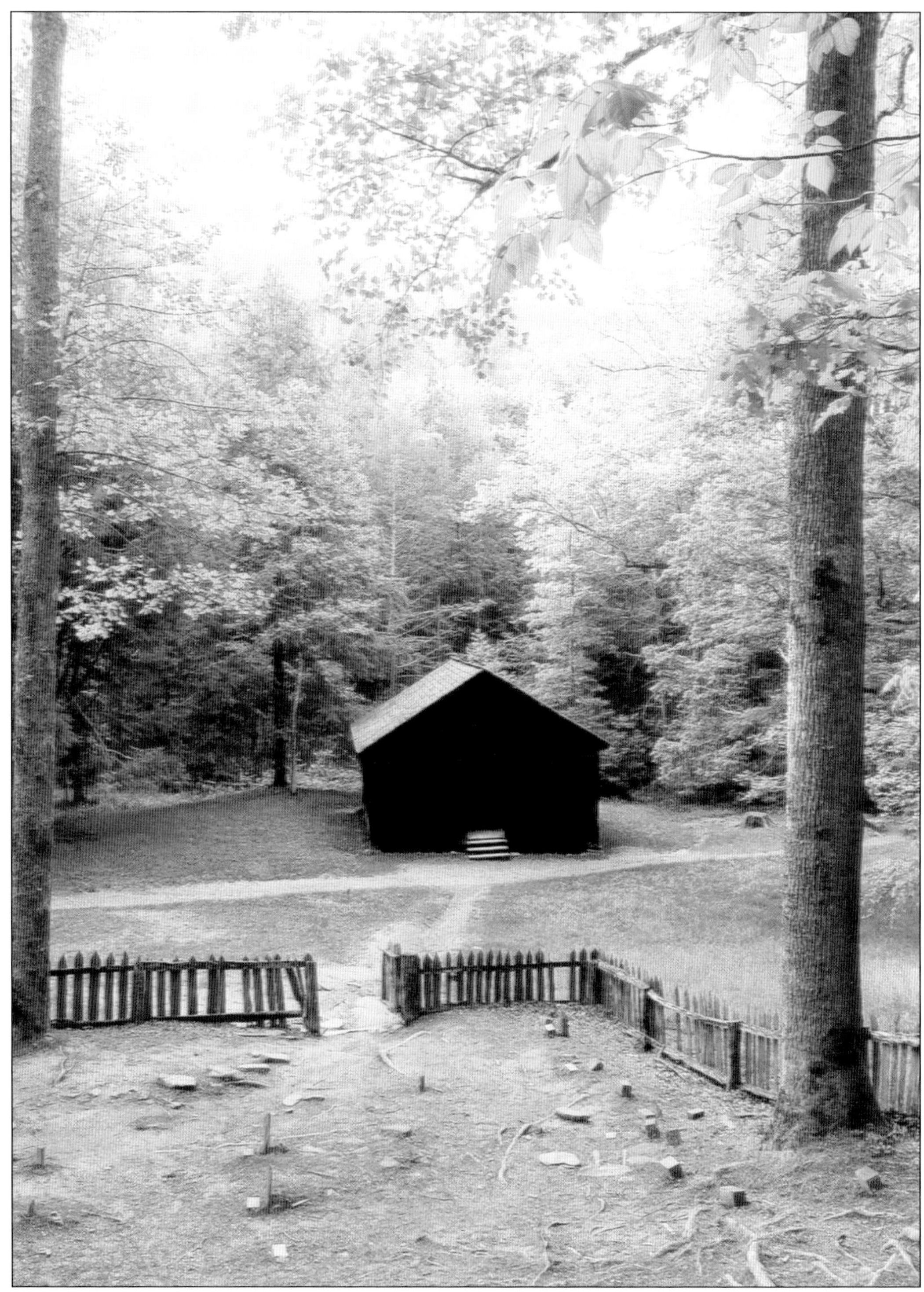

The Little Greenbrier Cemetery is extremely eroded even after many attempts to rehabilitate it. The view from this site includes Rocky Ridge in the background along with the school and cemetery. (Photograph by the author.)

Eight

Graffiti and Vandalism

Fools' names, like fools' faces, are often seen in public places.

According to the *New Oxford American Dictionary*, Graffiti is defined as writing or drawings scribbled, scratched, or sprayed illicitly on a wall or other surface in a public place. It seems that certain members of the public cannot resist the urge to write on federal property, much to the dismay of the National Park Service.

Vandalism is defined as the deliberate and malicious destruction of or damage to public, private, or government property. The main causes of this vary widely. Vandalism can be attributed to trying to be cool in a group of friends, being a "bad boy," or just being bored. Sometimes it is as elementary as posting "John loves Mary" for all to see.

Volunteers and the general public continue to turn in suspects to the park's law enforcement division for prosecution. Unfortunately, federal law cases are not published in the local newspaper as a deterrent to vandalism and graffiti.

According to the US Department of Justice, violations of regulations governing the use and maintenance of national parks could lead to imprisonment or fines.

One of the original benches from 1882 is still in the school. It remained free of graffiti until the late 2010s, when someone carved on it. The NPS fights an ongoing battle to remove what graffiti it can from the building. However, carvings deep in the wood will remain there indefinitely.

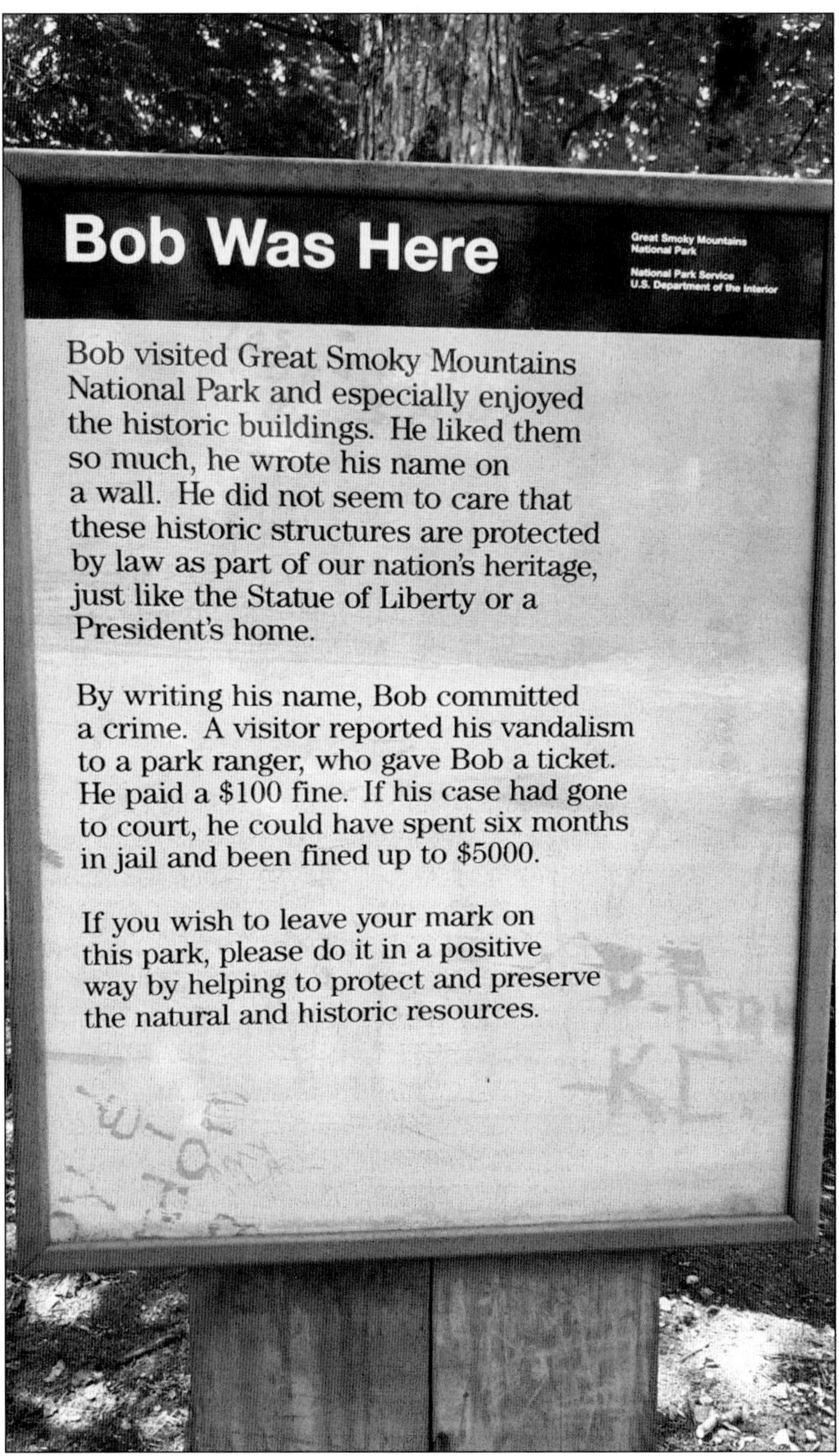

This sign outside the school states that vandalizing the building is a crime. Due to the absence of constant staff, graffiti and vandalism are constant problems. These signs are also posted at other historic structures in the park. (Photograph by the author.)

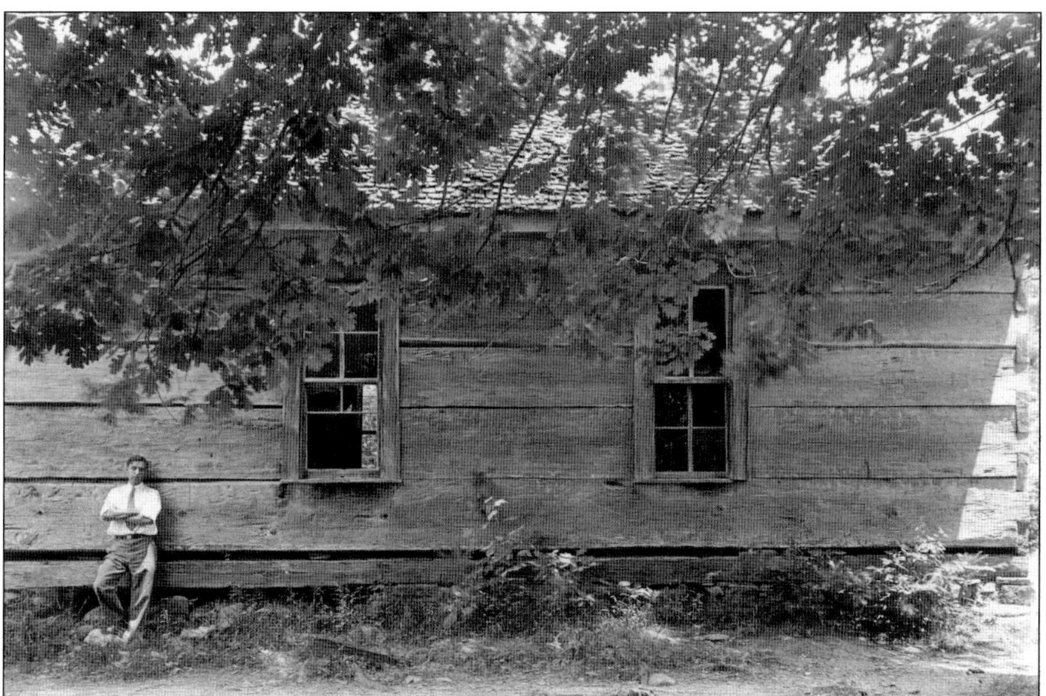

This is a photograph of the school as it looked around 1936, before the graffiti. Note the natural surroundings, as the yard was not mowed and the trees were not trimmed. (Courtesy Great Smoky Mountains National Park archives.)

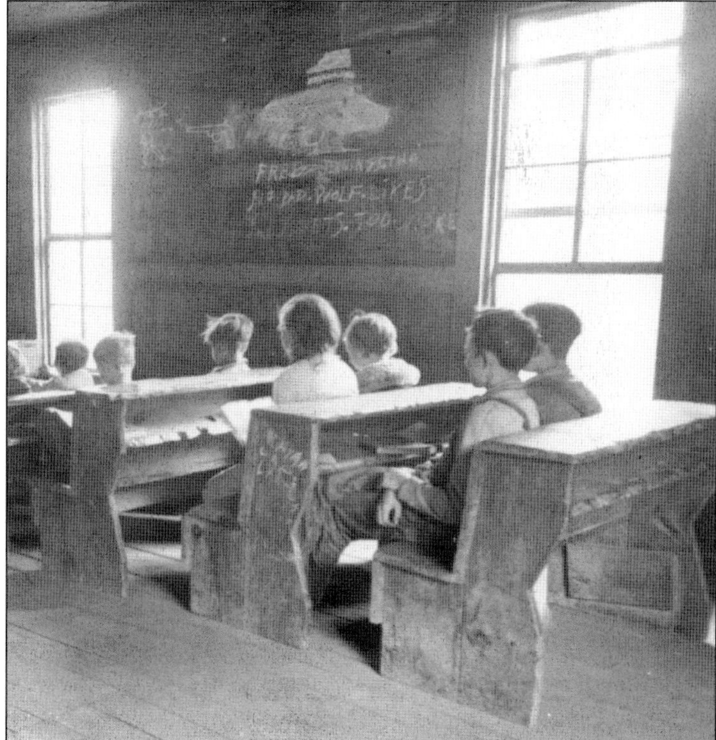

The graffiti on the wall in this photograph taken by E.E. Exline on March 2, 1936, reads, "Fred. Jennings. The Big.. Bad.. Wolf. Likes Cegarets. Too. Smoke." Several of the benches are the same ones still in the school today. (Courtesy Great Smoky Mountains National Park archives.)

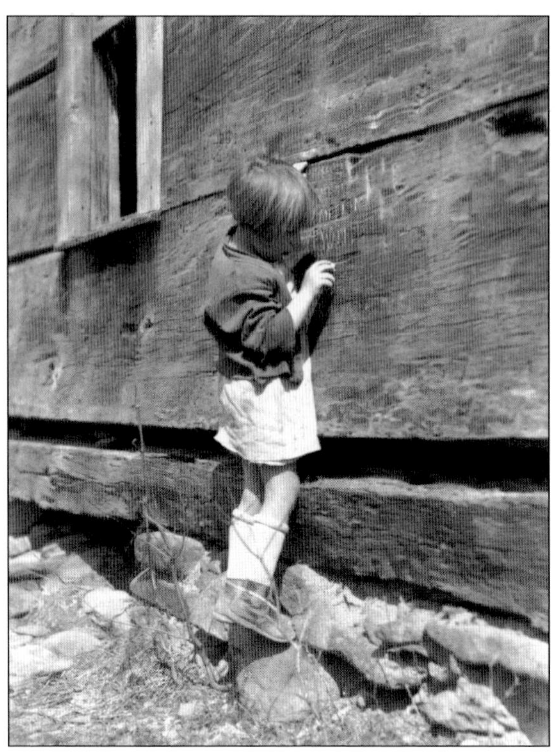

In this photograph taken by E.E. Exline on March 2, 1936, it appears that Margaret "Billy" Tallent may have been one of the building's original graffiti artists. Since this was the day the school closed, she possibly thought the building would be razed, so it is understandable why she would do this. (Courtesy Great Smoky Mountains National Park archives.)

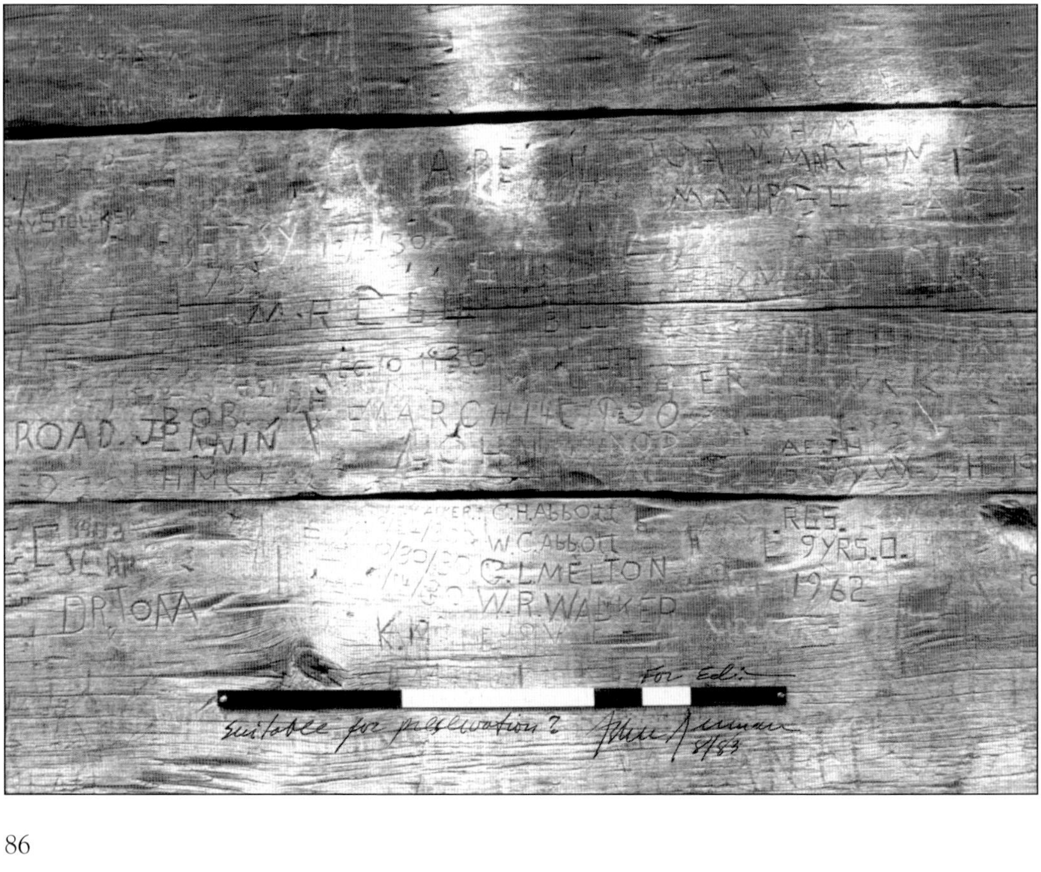

Graffiti is shown on one of the outside walls in 1983. It has only grown worse with the passage of years. (Courtesy Great Smoky Mountains National Park archives.)

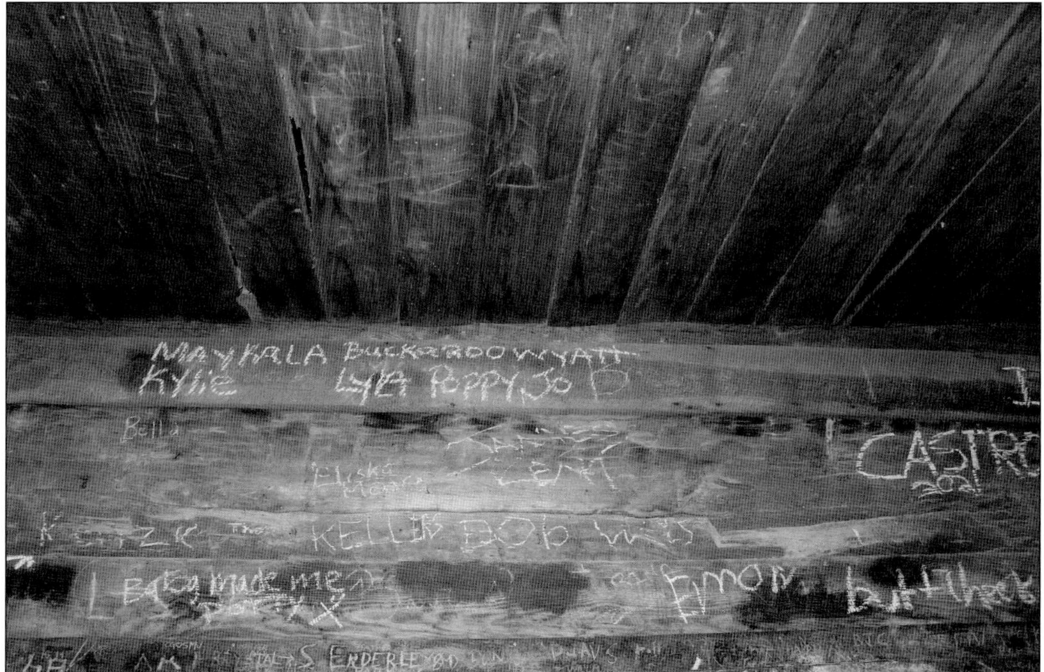

It must have taken some effort for these visitors to write their names so close to the ceiling. Luckily, chalk easily comes off of the wooden walls. (Photograph by the author.)

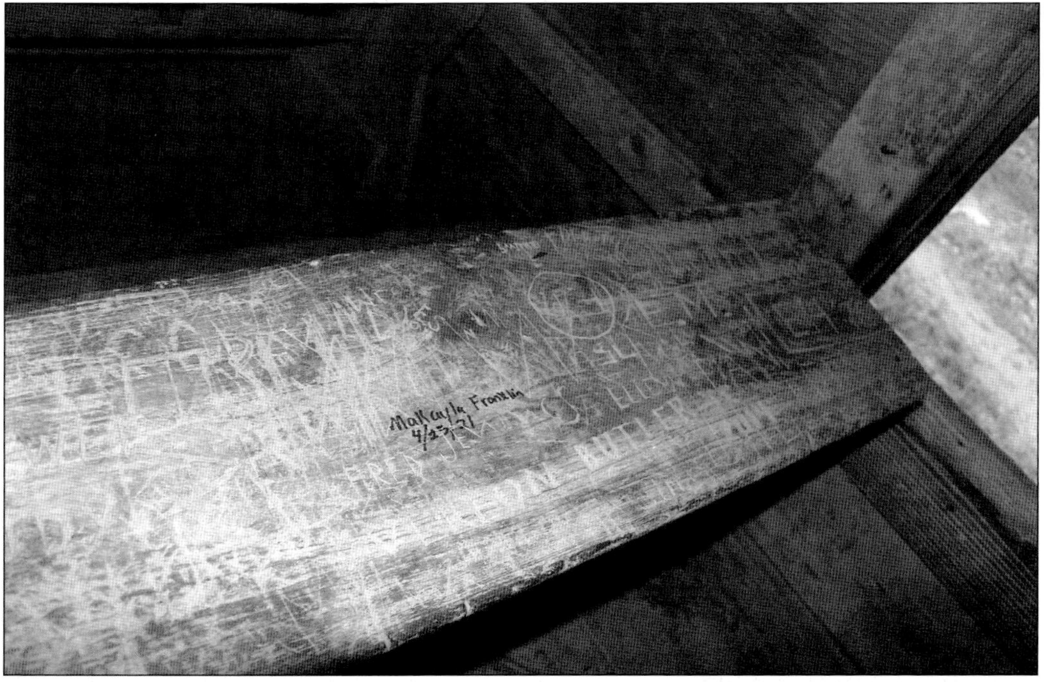

After remaining pristine for more than 130 years, the original bench from 1882 is now defaced with carvings, ink, and chalk. Without constant supervision of the building, such acts will only increase with time. (Photograph by the author.)

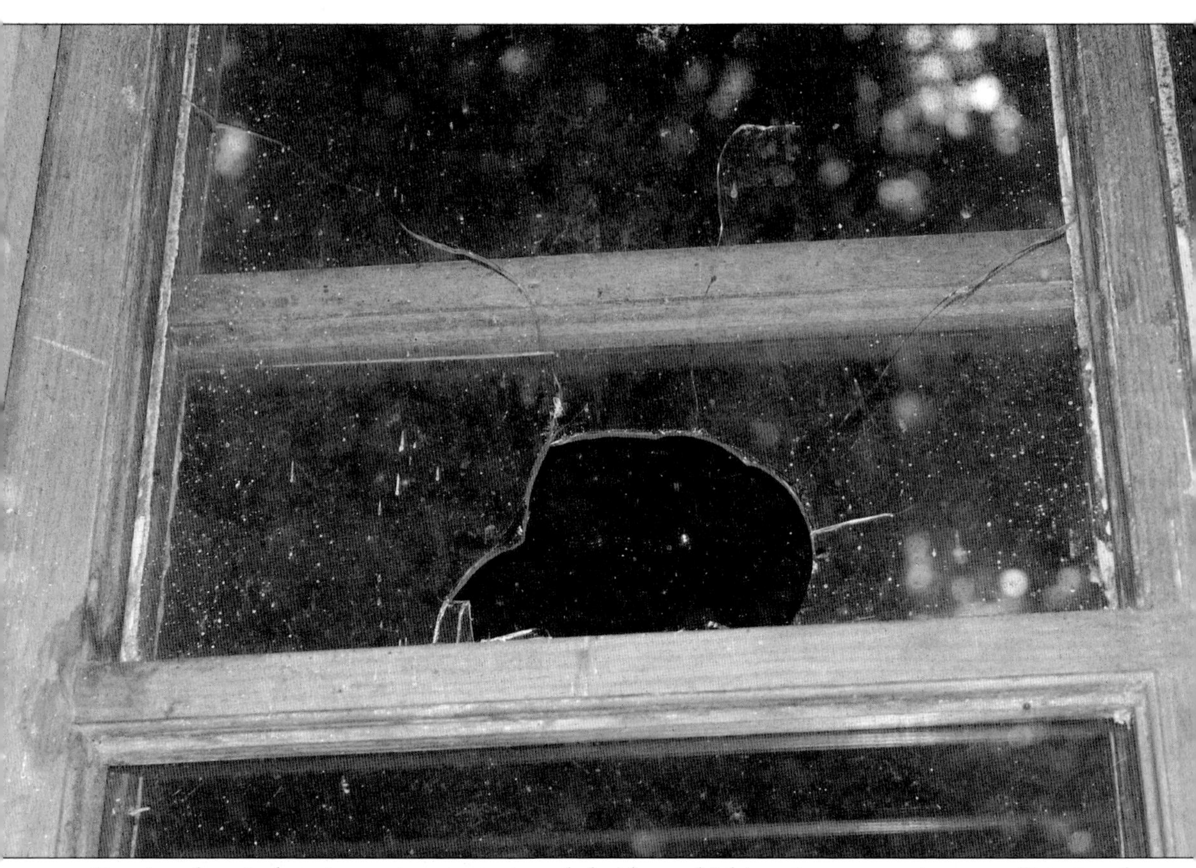

Keeping the windows intact is a constant task for the park's historic preservation crew. Repairs of such vandalism have to wait for several weeks to months because of the small number of people on the crew, which is charged with taking care of over 90 historic structures throughout Great Smoky Mountains National Park. In 2013, the park had only three or four permanent positions for specialists who were trained in historic preservation techniques. (Photograph by the author.)

Nine

The Future of Little Greenbrier

Hopefully, Great Smoky Mountains National Park and Little Greenbrier will live on for future generations. Repairs have been made to the Little Greenbrier School over the years, and surely more will take place as time goes by. With the passing of longtime program volunteers, it is hoped that the programs will be hosted by Walker family members or other people from the community. If not, other volunteers will rise to the occasion to continue this tradition.

The Little Greenbrier School was listed in the National Register of Historic Places in 1973. Under the register's guidelines, no alterations may be made to the building, and no improvements should be made except for general upkeep.

The Little Greenbrier School/Church has been a meeting place for the descendants of those who originally made their homes in the area about 200 years ago. Many generations of their descendants still live near the area outside the park's boundaries and return to the school regularly. They and tens of thousands of park visitors have happened upon this special place and been touched by the spiritualism and comforting aura of the Little Greenbrier community.

As long as Great Smoky Mountains National Park exists, so should the Little Greenbrier School. If the land ever reverts back to nature, so be it—it will be as the first settlers found it.

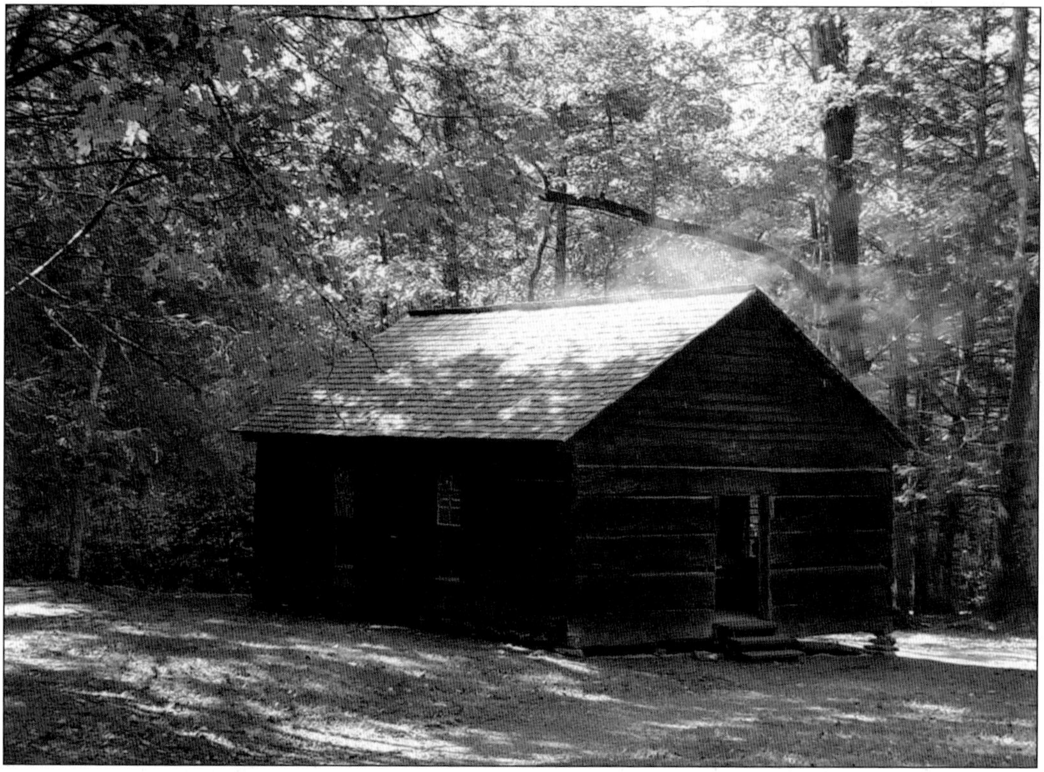

After a fall rain, steam comes off the roof of the school. The roof has been replaced numerous times over the building's many years. (Photograph by the author.)

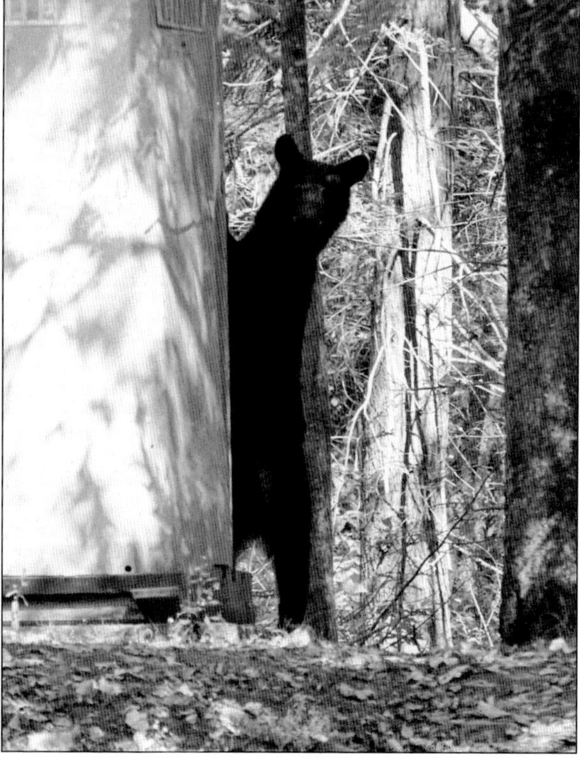

A black bear visited the portable bathroom in the late 2010s. Bears make themselves at home at Little Greenbrier, as there are numerous oak trees producing acorns for the bears to eat. (Author's collection.)

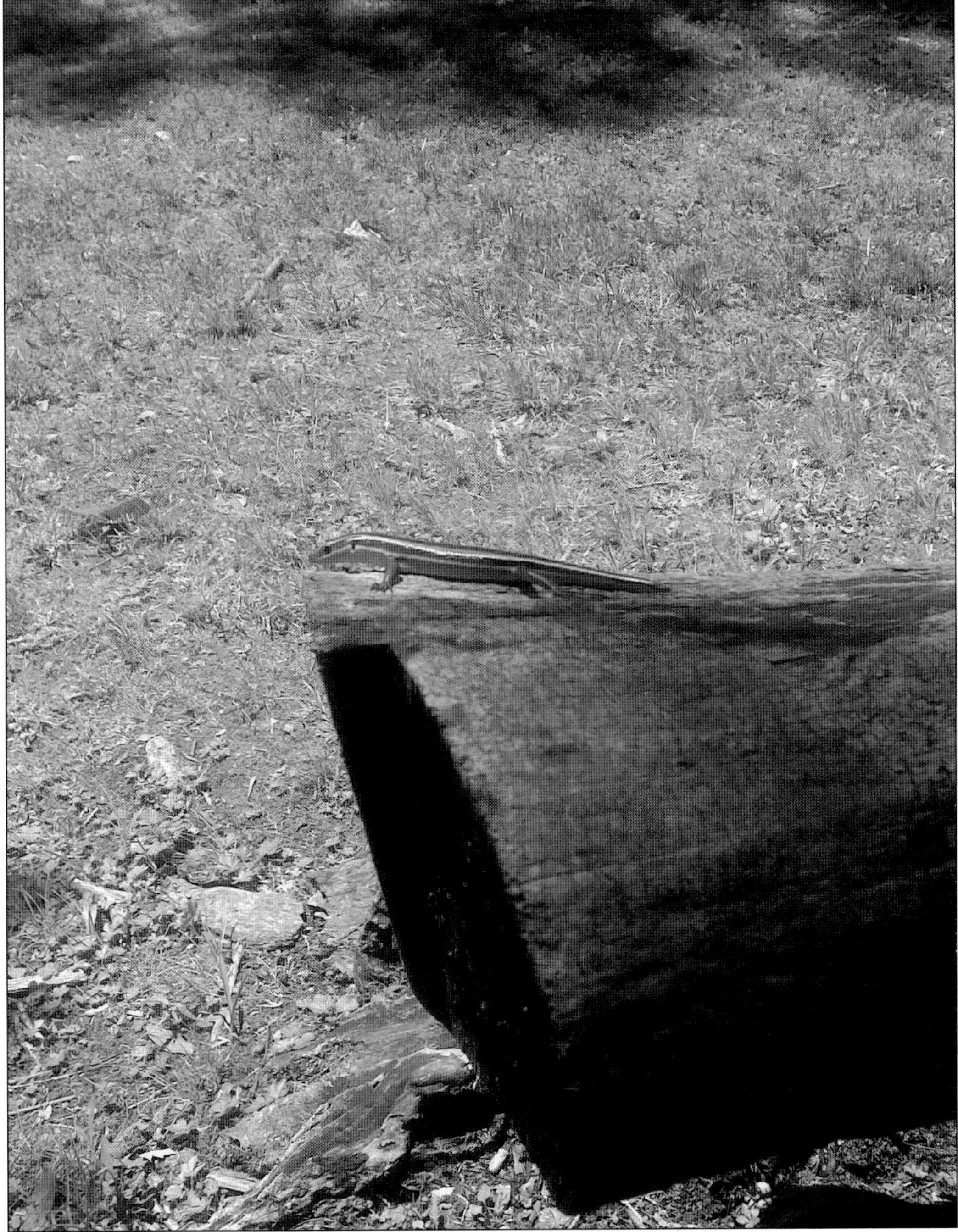

Blue-tailed skinks have the run of the place when no one is around. The male skinks have blue tails, while the females are rather dull in color. (Photograph by the author.)

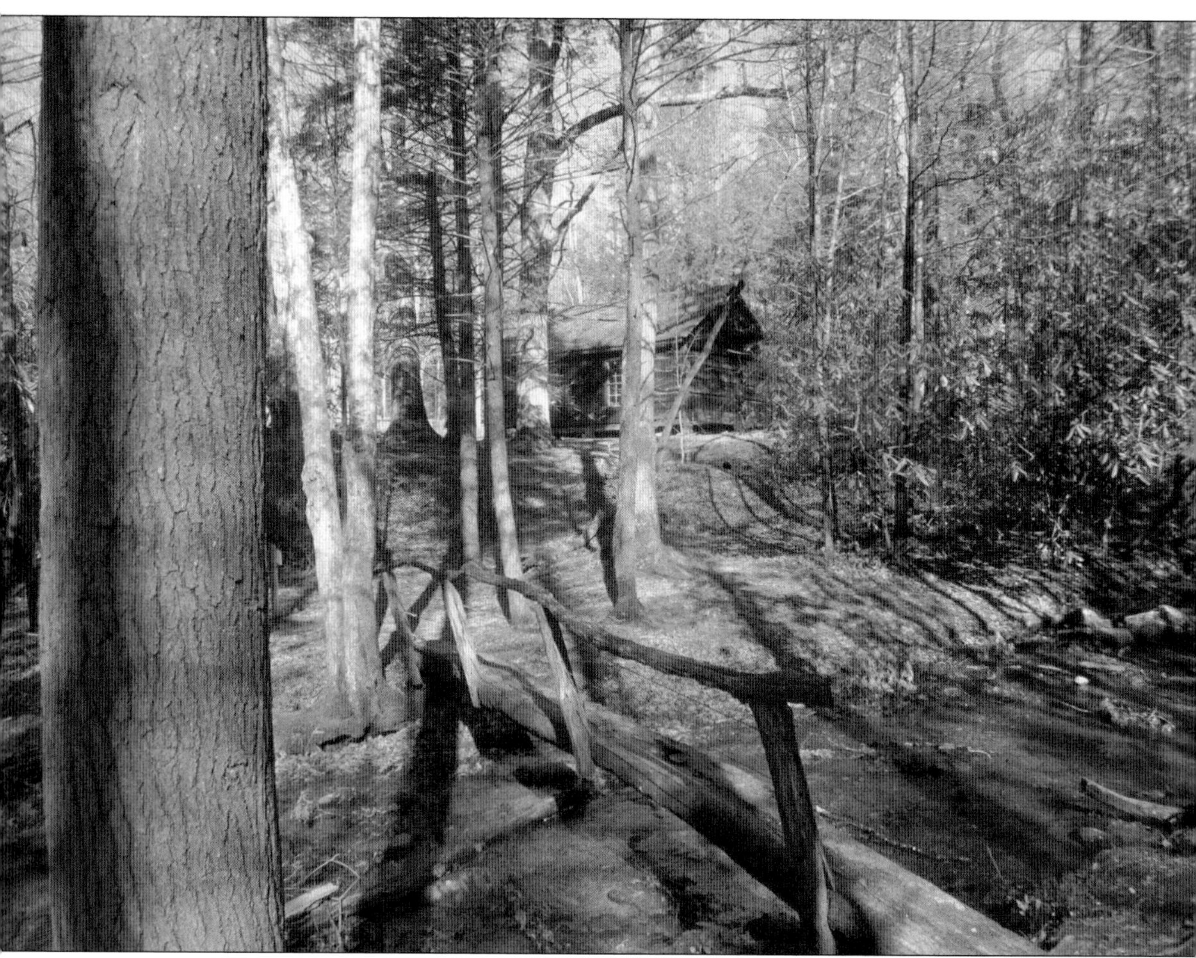

The hiking trails to the Little Greenbrier School will retain their trail status in the future for walking adventurers. This view is from the trail starting at Metcalf Bottoms and ending at the Little Greenbrier School. (Photograph by the author.)

Teachers of the Little Greenbrier School

Richard Perryman, two terms, 1882–1883
James B. Lawson, two terms, 1884–1885
Joan Wear, two terms, 1886–1887
John Lawson, two terms, 1888–1889
Sydna Myers, one term, 1890
Robert Rambo, one term, 1891
Joan Wear, one term, 1892
Callie Whaley, one term, 1893
Mitchell McCarter, one term, 1894
George Emert, one term, 1895
Levi McCarter, one term, 1896
John Henry Walker, three terms, 1897–1899

(The school was closed in 1900.)

John Henry Walker, one term, 1901
Josie Ogle, one term, 1902
John S. Porter, one term, 1903
Dave McCarter and Cora Bryan, one term, 1904
J.W. McCarter, one term, 1905
Ana Ogle, one term, 1906
Malinda King, one term, 1907
Stewart Lawson/Louia Abbott, one term, 1908
Malinda King, one term, 1909
Pearl Hastings, one term, 1910
Harkless Ogle, one term, 1911
Laura Roberson, one term, 1912
Hester Headrick, one term, 1913
Georgia Webb, one term, 1914
Harkless Ogle, one term, 1915
Lula King, one term, 1916
Harkless Ogle, two terms, 1917–1918
Malinda King, one term, 1919
Zula Scott, one term, 1920
Maud Marine, one term, 1921
Walter Ogle, one term, 1922
Othie Myers, one term, 1923
Fred Clark, one term, 1924
Howard Bailey, one term, 1925
Alice Huskey, one term, 1926
Ray Shrader, one term, 1927
Alice Huskey, one term, 1928
Myrtle Patty, one term, 1929
Julie Carnes, one term, 1930
Molly Clabo, one term, 1931
Alma King Headrick, one term, 1932
Alverta King, one term, 1933
Myrtle Brewer, one term, 1934
Herman Matthews, one term, 1935

Residents Interred in Little Greenbrier Cemetery

Original Marked Graves

Infant son of Mr. and Mrs. Ernest Walker, January 15, 1929

Edith Walker (daughter of John H. and Mary Walker), September 10, 1920–July 4, 1925

Infant daughter of J.H. and Mary Walker, born August 11, 1912

Roy Thomas Walker (son of J.H. and Mary Walker), January 19, 1919–July 31, 1919

Irene Walker (daughter of J.H. and Mary Walker), November 19, 1922–June 20, 1925

Infant son of J.T. and I.A. Walker, born and died September 11, 1900

William Earl Walker (son of Tom and Josie Moore Walker), August 23, 1933–October 6, 1933

Nora Stinnett (daughter of Mr. and Mrs. Ben Stinnett), November 1, 1921–August 2, 1923

Peggy Stinnett Hicks (wife of Will Hicks; daughter of Henry and Mary Wilkerson Stinnett), 1884–1924

Meliccie Cross Wilkerson (wife of Jim Wilkerson), died September 1, 1893

Fieldstones

Hattie Heaton

Carl Jones (a hired hand traveling through when he worked on the section of the railroad)

Infant Jennings (Westly Jennings, infant son of Smith and Martha Ann Jennings)

Perry Jennings

Robert Wesley Oliver (son of Carey and Ida Ellen Stinnett Oliver), born and died November 11, 1918

Geneva Brown (daughter of Obe and Esther Brown)

Infant Turner (infant of Mary Turner)

Burt Moore

Will Moore (son of Burt Moore)

Giles Sherman Walker (son of James Thomas and Ida Ann Stinnett Walker)

Daniel Westley Walker (son of James Thomas and Ida Ann Stinnett Walker)

James Allen Shelton (half-brother to Jim Shelton)

Sam Stinnett (son of Manning and Lou Stinnett), June 22, 1912–April 18, 1920

Infant Stinnett (son of Jenry and Mary Stinnett)

Martha Ann Moore (daughter of Burt Moore)

Tom Wilkerson (son of Thomas and Margaret Wilkerson), born April 1869

Rachel Moore (mother of Burt Moore)

Mary Rebecca Stinnett (daughter of Bill and Clarinda Patterson Stinnett)

Martha Elizabeth Stinnett (daughter of Bill and Clarinda Patterson Stinnett)

Infant Abbott (son of Gilbert and Nancy Abbott)

Infant Metcalf (infant of Riley Metcalf)

Millie Stinnett

Ephraim Ogle

Unmarked Graves

Mary Ann Wallace (sister to Burt Moore)

Nancy Jennings (sister to Burt Moore; wife of Buck Jennings)

Parton baby (infant of Leander and Matt Moore Parton)

Alice Moore (daughter of Burt Moore)

Logan Turner (brother of George Turner)

Infant Huskey (infant of Jess and Jessie Moore Huskey)

Eurstel Stinnett (son of Lee and Reesie Sims Stinnett), born and died December 13, 1926

Infant Hicks (daughter of Will and Peggy Stinnett Hicks), born and died 1906.

Walter Stinnett (infant son of Raish and Anna Roberts Stinnett)

Nancy Stinnett (infant daughter of Raish and Anna Roberts Stinnett), July 20, 1932–November 26, 1933

Infant Stinnett (daughter of Ben and Callie Stinnett), born and died September 20, 1935

James Walter Walker (son of James Thomas and Ida Ann Stinnett Walker)

Salley Walker (daughter of James Thomas and Ida Ann Stinnett Walker)

Infant Walker (infant of James Thomas and Ida Ann Stinnett Walker)

Infant Walker (son of Wiley and Martha Jane Walker)

Andy Moore

Ogle Girl

Ogle Girl

Riley Metcalf

Infant Metcalf (infant of James and Rhoda Metcalf)

Infant Wilkerson (infant of Dan Wilkerson)

Tom Wilkerson Sr. (father of Tom Wilkerson Jr.)

Noah Ogle (brother to Margaret Ogle Stinnett)

Margaret Ogle Stinnett (sister to Noah Ogle)

Mary Ann Wallace's three babies